# OVERCOMER

## 25 Keys to Walking Victoriously

———

Aretha Grant

# *Overcomer*

Overcomer.
Copyright © 2018 by Aretha Grant.
All rights reserved. No portion of this book may be reproduced in any form without permission in writing from the publisher. Published by Aretha Grant, PO Box 150, Fairplay, MD 21733.
Visit our website at www.arethagrant.com

Printed in the United State of America

Unless otherwise indicated, all Scripture quotations are taken from the King James Bible.

Also used: New American Standard Bible

Also used: New International Version

ISBN-13: 978-0-692-06065-0
ISBN-10: 0692060650

# 25 Keys to Walking Victoriously

## *Dedication*

This book is dedicated to all my beautiful Sisters-in-Christ who don't yet know they are Overcomers. I'm cheering for you my Sisters. Stand on the Word of God and BELIEVE Him.

This book is also dedicated to every woman ever diagnosed with breast cancer. You are my she-ros. You are Overcomers. You are more than Conquerors.

# *Overcomer*

## *Acknowledgements*

I want to thank the Father, the Son, and the Holy Spirit without whom I wouldn't have learned these wonderful lessons.

Thank you to my husband, Andre, and children, Joshua, Alex, and Charis. Thank you for your patience as I wrote this and many other books. Thanks for entertaining all my "book ideas".

Thank you to all my family, especially my sister Daisey Matthews and my brother Mark Dorsey. Thank you for stepping up to the plate and parenting this hard-headed, wayward child. I love you to LIFE!

Thank you to Pastor Mitch and Lady Alissa Robinson, and Great Commission Ministries for your encouraging words and gentle reminders to keep writing. I love my church! "There's a Bible lesson in that."

Thank you to Bishop Paul E. Kemp, my father in the Gospel (formerly of Sanctuary Progressive Ministries, Frederick MD), Bishop Ross Jackson (West Falls Christian Community Church, Mt. Airy, MD), Bishop Jay Williams (Grace Tabernacle Ministries, Frederick, MD), and Bishop Al Smith (formerly of Word of Life Outreach Ministries, Williamsport, MD). Your prayers and answers to ALL my questions are more appreciated than you'll ever know.

## 25 Keys to Walking Victoriously

Thank you, Vanessa Robinson, editor extraordinaire, a God-sent angel who helped make my dream a reality. Thanks to everyone who reads this book. I consider it an honor you would read my book when so many awesome books are already written on the topic. You could have chosen any book but you chose mine and I'm forever grateful.

Anthony, Mommy, and Michael, I pray you were proud of me…

# Overcomer

## Table of Contents

| | |
|---|---|
| ***INTRODUCTION*** | **8** |
| ***KEY 1 - LUKE 7:6-7,9*** | **14** |
| ***KEY 2 - JAMES 1:22*** | **22** |
| ***KEY 3 - 2 CORINTHIANS 12:9-10*** | **26** |
| ***KEY 4 - PROVERBS 3:5-6*** | **30** |
| ***KEY 5 - ROMANS 8:28*** | **34** |
| ***KEY 6 - ROMANS 8:37*** | **38** |
| ***KEY 7 - PSALM 34:1-3*** | **44** |
| ***KEY 8 - LUKE 8:48*** | **49** |
| ***KEY 9 - HEBREWS 11:1*** | **53** |
| ***KEY 10 - PHILIPPIANS 3:13*** | **58** |
| ***KEY 11 - MATTHEW 6:14*** | **64** |
| ***KEY 12 - ROMANS 12:2*** | **70** |
| ***KEY 13 - 1 CORINTHIANS 15:10*** | **75** |
| ***KEY 14 - ROMANS 8:14*** | **80** |
| ***KEY 15 - PHILIPPIANS 4:6-7*** | **87** |
| ***KEY 16 - ISAIAH 26:3*** | **92** |
| ***KEY 17 - ISAIAH 54:17*** | **98** |
| ***KEY 18 - EPHESIANS 6:12*** | **105** |
| ***KEY 19 - ISAIAH 61:3*** | **110** |
| ***KEY 20 - 2 TIMOTHY 1:7*** | **117** |

## 25 Keys to Walking Victoriously

| | |
|---|---|
| **KEY 21 - PSALM 23:4** | **131** |
| **KEY 22 - JOB 2:10** | **136** |
| **KEY 23 - ISAIAH 40:31** | **141** |
| **KEY 24 - 1 PETER 5:7** | **146** |
| **KEY 25 - ACTS 28:5** | **151** |
| **CLOSING WORDS** | **160** |

# *Overcomer*

## INTRODUCTION

*"Ye are of God, little children, and have overcome them: because greater is He that is in you, than he that is in the world," (1 John 4:4)*

I am in remission from stage 2A invasive ductal carcinoma breast cancer at the time of this writing.

On October 22, 2013, I received my diagnosis and subsequently underwent sixteen rounds of chemotherapy, a lumpectomy of the left breast, and thirty-three rounds of radiation therapy. (After follow-up mammograms and discussions with the oncologist and surgeon, the lump remaining in my left breast is nothing more than scar tissue. I consider the lump my battle wound, my badge of courage, and my reminder of what I've overcome).

I've faced cancer and the feelings cancer brought into my life, and by the grace of God, lived to tell my story. I'm an overcomer. And although I believe calling myself an overcomer is presumptuous, the Lord prompted me to type, so I typed - OVERCOMER.

# 25 Keys to Walking Victoriously

To overcome in 1 John 4:4 means to subdue (literally or figuratively), conquer, prevail, get the victory[1]. Frankly, I've faced, and had to overcome, many challenges. I've had to conquer situations. I've had to prevail. And I've had to get the victory over dire circumstances. How was I able to overcome the challenges I've faced? I overcame through Jesus Christ.

Although the phrase is cliché - I can honestly declare, "If it had not been for the Lord who was on my side…" As far back as I can remember, the Lord has been on my side, even preceding salvation. He held my hand, ordered my steps, and redirected me when I ventured to the broad path leading to destruction.

Three months after my high school graduation, my preemie son, Anthony, passed away at the tender twenty-two months old. November of the same year, I turned eighteen; four months later my mother passed. I was depressed and distraught over the loss of my son and my mother. Clouds of loneliness and depression followed me like a shadow. The hurt from losing two of the people dearest to me and loved me most was intensified by guilt and shame. I was 18 years old, depressed, distraught, guilty, and

---

[1] Strong's Numbers G3528

ashamed. Then I met a man who came along telling me all the things I wanted and needed to hear. I was wounded and looking for love. I eventually got pregnant and married him. The marriage lasted three years.

Anger and bitterness toward him and my plight, enlarged my downward spiral. I was emotionally and financially bankrupt. The short version - I was a hot mess. Fortunately for me, this low place was where Jesus Christ began knocking at the door of my heart. Although it wasn't evident then, I was exactly where I needed to be.

During my downward spiral, my father, stepmother, and sister accepted Christ, began attending church, and talking to me about the Lord. My father bought my first Bible in December 1989. I liked the Bible stories and sporadically attended church with them. However, I wasn't ready to accept Jesus as my Lord and Savior. I was interested in what I was learning about Jesus but not interested enough to commit my life to Him. I wanted the knowledge without knowing the Giver of the knowledge. Besides, I thought church was for boring, old people and I was still young and wanted to have fun. And so, I continued living my way.

# 25 Keys to Walking Victoriously

At this point, I started drinking. I wasn't overindulging in alcohol. I drank just enough to numb my pain. Amid this emotional chaos, I was attending church occasionally and reading my Bible almost every day. The more I read my Bible, the more I realized my lifestyle wasn't pleasing to God, and I needed to make a change. Changing was difficult because I didn't trust the God I heard about in church.

I had an encounter with the Lord in 1999 which set me up for change. I remember the moment I felt God's love for me. I don't write well enough to articulate what I felt that day. I experienced a love, joy, and peace I'd never felt before. God's love changed from an abstract idea I'd read in the Bible, to something I could actually feel, know, and experience. And I LOVED experiencing His love for me. But the fullness of God's love had to break through the depression, guilt, shame, anger, bitterness, and emptiness planted over the years. Overcoming them took time.

The Lord is still taking me through the healing and restoration process, a process my soul desperately needs. After all these years, the residue of my past is still with me in some areas. However, I believe a part of our breakthrough is the realization or awareness that we will always need the Lord's help. We will never outgrow His assistance, mercy, or grace.

## *Overcomer*

The more I grow in my relationship with the Lord, the more I realize my dependence upon Him.

God started healing and delivering me by introducing Himself to me as Abba. I sought God early and communed with Him often. I communicated with Him as a daughter communicates with her father. I poured out my heart to Him and sought Him on a variety of topics. Today, prayer is one of my favorite spiritual disciplines. Communing with Abba is neither a burden nor a chore to me. I look forward to prayer as my intimate time with Him. If you're seeking a breakthrough, I urge you to get alone with God as often as you can. Pray and ask Him to heal you of the broken, hurting areas of your life; those areas no one can physically touch but where you feel pain.

Breakthrough also comes through applying the Word of God. Personal application is the primary objective of this book. Let me add my disclaimer: people can receive breakthrough and healing through various methods. God deals with each of us differently. And although I'm sure you can receive breakthrough without the Word of God (all things are possible), I believe the study and application of His word are vital, during and after breakthrough.

Take a journey with me as I share the scriptures the Holy Spirit used to help me overcome the hardships I've encountered

## 25 Keys to Walking Victoriously

and how the Word of God can help you overcome your tests and trials too. My prayer is you develop a love of, or increase your love of, the Word of God, and draw strength from my testimony and the 25 Keys I've included for you. I AM an "Overcomer" and I want you to realize you're an "Overcomer" too.

*Overcomer*

### KEY 1 - LUKE 7:6-7,9

**"Then Jesus went with them. And when He was now not far from the house, the centurion sent friends to Him, saying unto Him, Lord, trouble not thyself: for I am not worthy that thou shouldest enter under my roof: Wherefore neither thought I myself worthy to come unto thee: but say in a word, and my servant shall be healed…When Jesus heard these things, He marvelled at him, and turned Him about, and said unto the people that followed Him, 'I say unto you, I have not found so great faith, no not in Israel'."**

This story taught me an important lesson about the Word of God: It's POWERFUL. The Word of God needs only to be received and spoken in faith to perform and produce in our lives.

Many of you have probably read this story before. If you haven't, please take a moment to read Luke 7:1-10 and Matthew 8:5-13. To summarize the story, a centurion sent messengers to Jesus asking Him to heal his servant. Jesus was in route to the centurion's house when the centurion stopped Him saying Jesus didn't need to come to his home. He only needed to speak a word. The centurion's faith is what taught me the valuable lesson on the power of God's word.

As I stated earlier, everyone is different. Everyone is different because our level of faith varies. Some people need to have someone anoint them with oil, while others need to have someone lay hands on them. The centurion simply needed Jesus to speak a word. My spirit quickened when I read this story. I needed and wanted the centurion's kind of faith.

Since reading the centurion's story, my faith says, "God, if you can give me a word from the Bible, I can be healed, comforted, delivered, etc." I seek a word from the Bible for everything I'm facing. Upon receiving my cancer diagnosis, I sought a word from the Bible. When I'm hurting, or offended, I seek a word from the Bible. When I need to make a major decision, I seek a word from the Bible. When I'm confused and need wisdom, I seek insight and clarity from the Bible. I believe with all my heart everything I need, every "word" of healing, deliverance, breakthrough, or restoration is in the Bible. Let's take a closer look at the centurion's faith in this story.

The centurion was an officer in the Roman army. He was not Jewish. He was not one of the children of Israel. He was a Gentile, and he BELIEVED. God doesn't consider our backgrounds or pedigrees. He considers our faith. Our faith is what pleases Him (see Hebrews 11:6).

Secondly, the centurion knew to whom to go for healing. I often go to family and friends first about my problems and go to God as a backup. God doesn't want to be our backup. He wants us to seek Him first in everything (Matthew 6:33). He wants to be our first thought. When we put Him first, He gives us what we need.

The centurion came to Jesus on behalf of his servant. Now, I don't see anywhere in scripture the servant asking the centurion to speak to Jesus on his behalf. I also don't see anywhere in scripture the servant knew the centurion was going to Jesus. Perhaps he did, but the scriptures are silent on this. So, I'm going to look at the story for what it says. The belief that people have to be a part of a prayer is false (think about unbelievers and those in comas). I believe the centurion's faith, not his servant's, brought about healing. This selfless act of faith describes the role of an intercessor.

Romans 8:34 teaches us Christ is at the right hand of the Father making "intercession" for us. Intercession means, to confer with, to entreat, deal with. Biblical usage of the word includes to go to or meet a person, esp. for the purpose of conversation, consultation, or supplication[2].

The centurion made intercession for his servant. We too can make intercession for others. Don't stop asking the Lord to heal, save, or deliver your family, friends, co-workers, or enemies.

When Jesus told the centurion he would heal his servant, the centurion responded by saying, *"...Lord, I am not worthy that thou shouldest come under my roof..."* (see Matthew 8:8). I'm always amazed when I hear people say they don't go to church, pray, or read the Bible because they don't feel worthy. Listen, none of us are worthy. We are only made worthy by the blood of Jesus Christ. Although the centurion felt unworthy, his feelings didn't stop him from going to Jesus for what he needed, and our feelings shouldn't stop us either.

In the same verse in which the centurion said he wasn't worthy, he showed faith in the power of God's word when he said, *"...but speak THE word only*, and my servant shall be healed," (emphasis mine). What's "THE" word he's talking about? The centurion needed Jesus to speak a word of healing.

---

[2] Strong's Numbers G1793

## *Overcomer*

The centurion came to Jesus in expectation, in hope, and so should we.

*"Therefore, I say unto you, What things soever ye desire, when ye pray, believe that ye receive them, and ye shall have them," (Mark 11:24).*

The centurion believed which is why he could declare to Jesus that his servant would receive healing if Jesus spoke a word. Do we believe? If not, then we certainly need to!

The centurion understood the power contained within the words of someone with authority. He understood Jesus was the ultimate authority and every principality, illness, and spirit are in subjection to Him. The centurion knew if Jesus spoke THE word of healing, the spirit of infirmity would have to flee from his servant.

Matthew 8:10 states Jesus heard the centurion's faith, marvelled, and told him, *"...verily I say unto you, I have not found so great faith, no, not in Israel."* Jesus commended the Roman officer for his belief in Him and His authority. The centurion's faith is what compelled Jesus to move on the servant's behalf. Later in verse 13, Jesus told the centurion,

*"...go thy way; and as thou hast believed, so be it done unto thee. And his servant was healed in the selfsame hour."*

What are we believing when we go to the Lord in prayer, when we go to Him for THE word? Jesus told the centurion, *"...Go; it shall be done for you as you have believed,"* (NASB version of verse 13). The Message Bible version is clearer: *"...Go. What you believed could happen has happened..."* The word "believe" in Matthew 8:13 means, to have faith (in, upon, or with respect to, a person or thing), i.e., credit; by implication, to entrust (especially one's spiritual well-being to Christ); commit (to trust), put in trust with.[3]

The centurion entrusted his servant to Jesus. He BELIEVED Him. Are we willing to entrust ourselves, our families, jobs, ministries, health, everything to God? Will we commit ourselves and our concerns to Him? When we entrust everything to the Lord, we're showing faith in Him, and He will move on our behalf. And sometimes He will move quickly.

*"And they that were sent, returning to the house, found the servant whole that had been sick," (Luke 7:10).*

---

[3] Strong's Numbers G4100

## *Overcomer*

Because of his faith, Jesus did exactly what the centurion asked of Him. The centurion asked Jesus to heal his servant, and Jesus healed him. I've asked Jesus to heal my hurts, to deliver me from incorrect, unclean, wicked thinking. I've asked the Lord to give me boldness in Him. I've asked Him to increase my confidence in who He created me to be. He has done that and much, much more because He is faithful and because I asked Him in faith. He wants to help us. If you don't know the Lord desires to help you, you won't expect anything from Him. This is where studying the word of God, the Bible, helps us build our expectations. When we're going through difficult times, like the centurion and his servant, we can pray, "Give me the Word, Lord, and healing, deliverance, help, and salvation will be my portion."

In my experience, God always gives me THE word I need for my situation. When I was facing chemotherapy for breast cancer, I was more afraid of chemo than of cancer. The day before my first infusion, I was a nervous wreck. I said, "Lord, I can't take the chemo until I hear from you." I remember opening my Bible and seeing, *"For God hath not given us the spirit of fear; but of power, and of love, and of a sound mind,"* (2 Timothy 1:7). God gave me the "word" I needed, dissected the verse, and made the word applicable to my specific fear (more on this in a later chapter). He gave me instructions based on the verse, and I followed them. I walked into each infusion appointment full of confidence, not in myself, my doctors, nor the nurses, but in God and THE word He gave me.

As the centurion needed a word and expected Jesus to help him, I too needed a word and expected Jesus to help me. Receiving a word and expecting Christ to move through the word is key to walking as an Overcomer. If you desire to overcome your circumstances, start seeking God for the word and His instructions on applying the word to your life.

*Overcomer*

### *KEY 2 - JAMES 1:22*

**"But be ye doers of the word, and not hearers only, deceiving your own selves."**

Anybody can read the Bible. Anybody can quote the Bible. But not everyone can apply biblical lessons to everyday living. If you want to walk as an Overcomer, you MUST apply biblical principles and teachings on a consistent basis. Let's take a closer look at James 1:22-25.

Thus far, I've written a great deal about applying the word of God to our lives. I cannot stress the importance of applying biblical principles because application of the Word makes all the difference in your ability to overcome the trials life throws at you. The Bible gives us the instructions we need to live victoriously. Deciding to heed those instructions is our choice. If we choose to disobey those instructions, we cannot blame God when we reap what we've sown out of disobedience.

## 25 Keys to Walking Victoriously

James 1:22 tells us when we're only hearers of the word, but not doers, we're deceiving ourselves. How can we expect to walk as Overcomers if we're walking in deception? Those who live victoriously, those who live abundantly, embrace and live in truth. They don't walk in deception; they aren't deluded or have delusional thinking. They see the truth and walk in the truth especially when it's difficult.

When someone hears the word of God but isn't a doer, the Bible says that person is like a man who looks at himself in a mirror but then forgets *"...what manner of man he was,"* when he walks away from the mirror. Application of the word helps us not to forget. Let me give you a natural example of this spiritual principle.

One of the best ways for me to know whether I understand an idea or concept is by trying to apply what I've learned. For instance, I had to learn new software for my job. I took some online training courses, traveled to California for four days of training, and then practiced in the database for a few weeks. However, I didn't know whether I could apply all the concepts I'd been taught to a real-world situation until I took the exam (I failed one part of the exam, by the way). And so, it is with us when we apply the word of God to our lives. As stated earlier in this chapter, anyone can hear, read, or quote the Bible but you

## *Overcomer*

won't know how spiritually strong you are until a situation arises in your life and you must apply what you've been reading, hearing, and quoting. Standing on the word of God is how you walk as an overcomer.

When you want to overcome adversity in any area of your life, know what the Bible says on the topic, seek out wise counsel, and apply what you've read and heard. You won't gain the victory until you DO what the Bible tells you to do. Until you DO what the Bible says, you're only a hearer of the word. We want to move away from being a mere hearer to being a doer of biblical principles.

*"But whoso looketh into the perfect law of liberty, and continueth therein, he being not a forgetful hearer, but a doer of the work, this man shall be blessed in his deed," (James 1:25).*

Let's look closer at verse 25. Imagine the Bible as a special mirror which shows you as you truly are, not the outward appearance, but your heart, your motives, your intentions, etc. This mirror shows what you're doing correctly but also shows areas in which you need improvement.

Now, imagine you look into this mirror and see hatred, animosity, bitterness, unforgiveness, hopelessness, despair, and doubt, walk away from the mirror and forget what you saw. If you've forgotten what you saw, you won't make any effort to change your behavior. You're only a hearer of the word.

Now, the same scenario, but instead of walking away from the mirror and forgetting what you saw, you take the necessary steps to change. You've now moved from being a simple hearer of the "word" to being a doer of the "work". The Bible declares this person will *"...be blessed in his deed."*

I find the use of the word "work" instead of "word" in verse 25 interesting. You see, the Bible isn't simply a bunch of words on a page in a book. The words in the Bible are powerful and *"alive and active and sharper than any two-edged sword,"* (see Hebrews 4:12). The words in the Bible provide instructions on the work we need to perform. When we perform the work, we are blessed.

Yes, overcoming obstacles requires work. When you seek the Lord for a word like the centurion, make sure you apply the word after you receive it. Applying the word will change your perspective and your life.

*Overcomer*

## KEY 3 - 2 CORINTHIANS 12:9-10

**"And He said unto me, 'My grace is sufficient for thee: for my strength is made perfect in weakness.' Most gladly therefore will I rather glory in my infirmities, that the power of Christ may rest upon me. Therefore I take pleasure in infirmities, in reproaches, in necessities, in persecutions, in distresses for Christ's sake: for when I am weak, then am I strong."**

If you want to change your life, and walk as an Overcomer, change your perspective. I cannot tell you how many times I've counseled beautiful, intelligent women who should be walking as Overcomers, but aren't because they can't change their perspective or their way of thinking. These women are stuck because they can't, or they refuse, to see their trials from God's perspective.

Let me make something abundantly clear right now: God isn't under any obligation to do what we want, when we want, the way we want. He's God, and we need to understand our lives belong to Him, and He has a purpose and plan for us. As I mentioned in a previous chapter, God will answer our prayers, but those prayers need to align with His will for our lives.

If you don't mind, let me go back to my cancer journey for a moment. Hearing the diagnosis devastated me. I was heartbroken because I viewed the diagnosis as either a curse from God or evidence He and I weren't as close as I thought we were. 2 Corinthians 12:8-10 is one of the scriptures the Lord gave me to overcome twisted thinking.

Paul says in verse 7 he was given a thorn in the flesh to buffet him. He prayed three times asking the Lord to remove the thorn from him. Theologians disagree on exactly what the "thorn" was. Notwithstanding, the thorn was something Paul had to deal with, something to humble him. Although the great Apostle Paul was working ministry and living holy, God didn't answer his prayer request the way Paul wanted. Paul wanted the thorn removed, yet Jesus answered his prayer saying, *"My grace is sufficient for thee: for my strength is made perfect in weakness,"* (see verse 9).

Paul didn't whine. He didn't complain. He didn't stop living holy or working ministry. Instead, Paul said, *"Most gladly therefore will I rather glory in my infirmities, that the*

## *Overcomer*

*power of Christ may rest upon me."* I had to make a similar declaration and change my perspective. I had to realize being diagnosed with cancer wasn't a curse, nor did my diagnosis mean God and I weren't close (I need to write about this one day). Perhaps God allowed me to be diagnosed with cancer so His strength could be *"made perfect"* in my weakness. Maybe I was diagnosed to glorify the Lord. Put another way, my diagnosis wasn't about me, but about Him. Maybe I was diagnosed to write and release this book. I could use my cancer journey to empower and inspire others to let the light of Christ shine through their situations and lives as well.

I had to declare with Paul that I would glory in my infirmity so Christ's power could rest upon me. And His power rested upon me indeed. Looking back on my journey now, I chuckle as I think about the people who couldn't believe I had cancer. Many people teased me saying, "Aretha, I refuse to believe you're going through cancer treatments." We would laugh and stand in awe of God because He truly kept me during that season. I never stopped working. On the contrary, I took my laptop to the chemo infusions so I could work. I often sat on conference calls while at my chemo appointments. I still preached and sang on the praise team as well. And for those who weren't told I had cancer, they didn't know until I publicized my diagnosis. The Lord empowered me to LIVE through that season of my life. Was my flesh afraid? Yep! Did I often wonder if I would die? Yep! Yet, the Holy Spirit told me to keep going, keep believing, keep living.

I learned to take pleasure in my infirmity, and I'm still learning to take pleasure in reproaches, necessities, persecutions, and distresses for Christ's sake because I now know when I am weak, I'm actually strong. The Overcomer takes pleasure in infirmities. Please understand I'm not saying an overcomer enjoys infirmities or welcomes them. Overcomers look for the lessons and the beauty in infirmities.

Understanding that our weaknesses don't make us weak but strong is one of the key ingredients in overcoming every hardship life throws our way. Indeed, leaning upon Christ's grace for strength doesn't make us weak, it makes us strong.

# *Overcomer*

## *KEY 4 - PROVERBS 3:5-6*

**"Trust in the Lord with all thine heart; and lean not unto thine own understanding. In all thy way acknowledge Him, and He shall direct thy paths."**

The previous chapter taught Overcomers that embracing Christ's grace for strength doesn't make them weak but strong. And if you want to walk as an Overcomer, you will need to lean and rely on the Lord as well.

I want you to think about an area in your life with which you've repeatedly struggled. The area could be your finances, your diet, your children, your job/career, your ministry, your spouse. The area could be anything. You keep seeing the same struggle repeatedly in your life.

You've prayed about it. You've tried to change. You've tried talking to the individual. You've tried talking to other people about the situation. You've gone to your Pastor about it. You're frustrated and out of patience. You're at your wit's end and ready to give up. You're a smart person, and shouldn't be experiencing so many problems because of this situation. What's going on? How can you fix this? How can you move beyond it? What's the problem? You've tried everything you know but still, see the same results.

God blessed each of us with a brain. We have the ability to think, reason, and deduce. We've used our brains since we were born and we're used to relying upon them. We are also blessed to possess women's intuition, a gut feeling which helps us judge situations and people and know how to navigate life's storms.

The problem with our brains and our intuition is they can be wrong. You see, Romans 12:2 tells us transformations comes through the renewing of our minds (more on this in a later Key). Our brains/minds have been in training since we were born and they've acquired some inaccurate information. This is why relying solely on our brains is a bad idea. The Bible gives us the help we need. Proverbs 3:5-6 comes to our rescue.

If you want to live the Overcomer's life, these verses should be in your arsenal. You should commit them to memory. When we come against daunting situations, we need to trust in the Lord. Trust means to be confident, sure; be bold, secure, put confidence, hope[4]. Unfortunately, many of us are quick to trust doctors, hospitals, medicine, lawyers, or our friends. We're slow to trust in the Lord. Proverbs 3:5 tells us to trust in Him with all the heart. God doesn't want to be our last resort. He wants to be our only resort.

The same verse also warns us against leaning to our understanding. Leaning to our understanding means we're supporting ourselves by what and how we understand. Our understanding is limited. We need the Holy Spirit to bring clarity, vision, and understanding. For example, when we are experiencing financial hardships, perhaps the way we rationalize causes us to rob Peter to pay Paul or maybe our understanding causes us to engage in illegal or illicit behavior to obtain the money we need. If we lean to our understanding, our behavior will put ourselves, our families, and homes at risk.

However, if we acknowledge God in everything we want to achieve, He will direct us. As I read my Bible, I see His directions always lead to victory, especially when what we see with the natural eye doesn't look like a victory (think Jesus on the cross). His directions don't always make sense to us, and so

---

[4] Strong's Numbers H982

we go back to what does make sense: our way of doing things, our understanding.

I've learned God's directions will lead you on an adventure. And believe me, God is anything but boring. I've also learned God doesn't always take us on a straight path. Sometimes you will encounter curves, hills, and valleys. God's directions aren't on a GPS and the journey on which He leads one person will be different from the journey of another person. God tailors His directions for each of us. He knows what we need on the journey. God knows what He wants to root out of us. He knows how He wants to change or transform us on the journey. He wants our testimonies of being Overcomers to glorify Him. Leaning to our understanding will not bring Him glory. Acknowledging Him and letting Him direct our paths will.

*Overcomer*

### KEY 5 - ROMANS 8:28

**"And we know that all things work together for good to them that love God, to them who are the called according to His purpose."**

This is my favorite verse. I've stood on Romans 8:28 many times and will continue to stand on it. Nowhere in this verse does God promise everything we go through will feel good to us, but He does promise they will work together for our good (for those who love God).

Why me? Why did I have to be the "1-in-8 women" to be diagnosed with cancer? I initially struggled with why. I questioned God, and I questioned myself. The diagnosis and subsequent chemotherapy treatments, surgery, radiation therapy, and skin burns certainly didn't feel good to me, but they have worked together for my good. Would I want to go through the journey again? Absolutely NOT!

## 25 Keys to Walking Victoriously

There's victory in this verse. There's hope in this verse. Those who stand on this verse and trust God to work everything together for their good will come out the other side of their challenges victorious.

Despite what you're facing right now, you are an Overcomer. You are victorious. How? Because if you love God and are called according to His purpose, then you are already an Overcomer. The thing you're going through will work together for your good. Overcomers understand this principle and always look with expectancy for the good in their trials and tribulations.

An Overcomer puts God's will, purposes, and plans before her comfort, wants, or agenda. An Overcomer knows her life isn't her own and will go through affliction which can glorify God.

*"And as Jesus passed by, he saw a man which was blind from his birth. And His disciples asked Him, saying 'Master, who did sin, this man, or his parents, that he was born blind?' Jesus answered, 'Neither hath this man sinned, nor his parents: but that the works of God should be made manifest in him," (John 9:1-3).*

We don't know how old this man was when he encountered Jesus, but we know he'd been blind since birth. Everyone knew

## *Overcomer*

him. He was a blind beggar. He couldn't have anticipated one day Jesus would come by and change his life. I'm sure he often asked the question, "Why me?"

Many of us wonder why we have to go through the afflictions and hardships we later need to overcome. The Christian life isn't one free of struggles, trials, or challenges. This life is one in which we face and overcome hardships, with His help. Indeed, struggles, trials, and challenges are opportunities for us to witness for Christ.

*"When He had thus spoken, He spat on the ground, and made clay of the spittle, and He anointed the eyes of the blind man with clay, and said unto him, 'Go, wash in the pool of Siloam,' (which is by interpretation, Sent). He went his way therefore, and washed, and came seeing. The neighbors therefore, and they which before had seen him that he was blind, said, 'Is not this he that sat and begged'?" (John 9:6-8).*

The man followed Jesus' instructions and people were astounded. They knew he was once blind; yet now he could see. They questioned his sight. Here was the moment of truth for the blind man. He could tell them what Christ had done and glorify the Lord, he could lie, or he could remain silent. This moment is where many of us fail the test because we are too afraid to tell others what Jesus did for us.

> *"He answered and said, "A man that is called Jesus made clay, and anointed mine eyes, and said unto me, Go to the pool of Siloam and wash: and I went and washed, and I received sight...whether He be a sinner or no, I know not: one thing I know, that, whereas I was blind, now I see'," (John 9:11, 25).*

I don't know everything about God, Jesus, the Holy Spirit, or the Bible, but this one thing I know: Everything I go through will work together for good because I will glorify God in everything I go through.

This man was born blind so *"...the works of God"* could be manifested in him. If he hadn't been born blind, God's works would not have been put on display the day Jesus restored his sight. Your trials and tests are presenting you with the same opportunity. Let God use you and them to manifest His works in the earth. Let your trials and tests work together for your good and God's glory.

# *Overcomer*

### *KEY 6 - ROMANS 8:37*

**"Nay, in all these things we are more than conquerors through Him that loved us."**

Overcomers are conquerors. Remember, the definition of overcome includes, "to subdue (literally or figuratively), conquer, prevail, get the victory." Overcomers become conquerors because they subdued, prevailed over, or got the victory over adversity. In other words, something has to arise requiring you to overcome or conquer it. If nothing ever arises, we'll never realize we are Overcomers.

I don't like drama. I don't like adversity nor spiritual warfare. However, I have to contend with them. Most people don't like these things, but they have to contend with them as well. Whether you're saved or not, you will have to confront drama, adversity, and spiritual warfare. They are a part of life. The Christian already has the victory though. We've already won. We need to trust in the Lord during the battle.

## 25 Keys to Walking Victoriously

To be more than a conqueror means we gain a decisive victory. The definition also means we more than conquer the obstacles life throws our way[5]. When we conquer something, we've subdued, dominated, or overpowered it. According to Romans 8:37, we are conquerors because of Jesus Christ.

When a challenge or obstacle comes our way, several options present themselves as well:

- We can run and not engage in the battle.
- We can surrender.
- We can stand on God's word and fight.

The choice is ours. However, for the Overcomer, there's one choice - stand and fight, according to God's instructions.

I've come across many Christians who would rather run or surrender. These options don't lead to victory. God doesn't get the glory in either of these options. Instead, we must stand and fight. We must persevere. We must endure to the end. We can't retreat, shrink back, or cower in the face of opposition. Too many people are depending upon us.

Looking back at the verse, something interesting which stood out to me is the Bible didn't only say we are conquerors.

---

[5] Strong's Numbers G5244

## *Overcomer*

The word "conqueror" would have been sufficient. Instead, the Bible says we are "more than" conquerors. If you look at the attributes of a conqueror, the Bible is saying we're more than those attributes. We are conquerors because we are in a fixed fight and Jesus has already won the victory for us.

In Psalm 23:4, David said:

*"Yea, though I walk through the valley of the shadow of death, I will fear no evil: for thou art with me; thy rod and thy staff they comfort me."*

Look at the first part again: *"...though I walk THROUGH..."*. The attitude of the Overcomer says, "I'm passing through this."

Unfortunately, some people think the challenge or obstacle is a permanent situation. How many times have you heard Christians say, "This too shall pass?" Well, it's true. Conquerors can't give up. They must maintain the mindset - this will pass because I'm passing THROUGH the valley. God will bring you out eventually.

Psalm 23 also teaches us we don't have to fear evil. Why? Whenever we face adversity or spiritual warfare, we have to remember Christ is with us. He has promised never to leave us nor forsake us. More than conquerors understand they are not in this battle alone, and the greater One is on their side. And His presence is what makes us more than conquerors.

This verse is one of the first verses the Holy Spirit spoke to my heart following my diagnosis. He told me I was more than a survivor. The Lord explained while many cancer survivors "remain alive or in existence," their quality of life, their joy, their peace diminishes. Cancer robs them of their sense of being. God told me I was more than a conqueror before I had my first chemo treatment, when I was still scared to death. I started speaking this verse over my life: "I am more than a conqueror"[6][7]. I spoke the verse when I didn't 100% believe what I was saying.

And you have to speak a word of victory now as well. You have to say what God says about you. You have to believe what God says about you even if you don't understand, see, or believe what you're saying. Conquerors place their faith in God and believe God will deliver them. Let's look at David.

David's father sent him out to the battlefield to take food to his older brothers. When he arrived and was speaking with

---

[6] Strong's Numbers G4100
[7] Breast cancer survivors on Facebook are urged to join my closed group at https://www.facebook.com/groups/breastcancerconquerors/

them, he witnessed Goliath issuing threats against the Israeli armies. David volunteered to fight Goliath, to his brothers' consternation. After David gave King Saul his qualifications, the king consented to send him to the battlefield where Goliath awaited. Goliath couldn't believe Israel would send such a scrawny man-child to fight him and said, *"...am I a dog, that thou comest to me with staves?"* Additionally, he said to David, *"Come to me, and I will give thy flesh unto the fowls of the air, and to the beasts of the field,"* (1 Samuel 17:43-44).

David didn't run in fear, retreat, nor did he cower. David stood boldly and confidently and said:

*"Thou comest to me with a sword, and with a spear, and with a shield: but I come to thee in the name of the Lord of hosts, the God of the armies of Israel, whom thou hast defied. This day will the Lord deliver thee into mine hand; and I will smite thee, and take thine head from thee; and I will give the carcasses of the host of the Philistines this day unto the fowls of the air, and to the wild beasts of the earth; that all the earth may know that there is a God in Israel," (1 Samuel 17:45-46).*

The Bible records David prevailed over Goliath by throwing a stone at him, sinking the stone into his forehead, subsequently killing Goliath.

David believed God. David had faith God would deliver Israel and God accomplished what David expected. The Overcomer believes God will deliver her. An Overcomer places her faith in God's word. Overcomers believe God is who He says He is and will accomplish what He says He will accomplish.

If you want to walk as an Overcomer, believe you are already more than a conqueror. Don't run from the battle. Stay on the battlefield, standing boldly and confidently, prevailing in the name of the Lord.

## *Overcomer*

### *KEY 7 - PSALM 34:1-3*

**"I will bless the Lord at all times: His praise shall continually be in my mouth. My soul shall make her boast in the Lord: the humble shall hear thereof, and be glad. O magnify the Lord with me, and let us exalt His name together."**

This is one of my favorite verses. While I quote the verse all the time, applying the verse is much more challenging. How does one bless the Lord at ALL times when faced with various challenges? How does one continually praise God when she's faced with multiple obstacles? How can you boast in the Lord when you're not sure God is going to come through in time? How can you magnify the Lord when you're having a plethora of problems and issues vying for your attention? No - putting these verses into action isn't easy but is absolutely necessary in the Overcomer's life.

David says to bless the Lord at all times. I don't see any conditions or contingencies on the statement. He doesn't say bless the Lord at all times if you feel like it or if you have enough money in the bank or if you're healthy or if your life is going well. Neither are we instructed to bless the Lord only when we're in our weekly church services. Indeed, he told us to bless the Lord ALL the time.

Overcomers have an attitude of praise. Overcomers can bless the Lord at all times because they don't focus on the problem but the problem-solver. Overcomers know God *"...is able to do exceeding and abundantly above all that we ask or think, according to the power that worketh in us,"* (see Ephesians 3:20). Overcomers aren't necessarily blessing the Lord for the problem. They're blessing the Lord for the help, the solution, the deliverance which are sure to come.

David went on to say God's praise will "continually" be in his mouth. Despite what you're facing or experiencing, learn to praise the Lord. Learn to praise the Lord in advance as Pastor Marvin Sapp sings in the song by the same name (Praise Him in Advance). Bring your praise into the church with you. Don't come to church and then wait for the praise and worship team to pump you up enough to praise the Lord. Psalm 100:4 instructs us to, *"Enter into His gates with thanksgiving, and into His courts with praise: be thankful unto Him, and bless His name."*

## *Overcomer*

Praise Him for who He is, for what He has done, and what He is going to accomplish.

Have you ever met someone who constantly talks about their problems? You could call them on the phone to catch up with them, and they'll spend the entire time talking about what they are going through in their lives. You can't add a word during the conversation. What would happen if the person changed their conversation to only boasting in the Lord? What would happen if the person talked about how God is going to move on their behalf? They would feel better and so would you.

David tells us in verse 2 that his soul will boast in the Lord. The Lord is the only person in whom we should boast. 1 Corinthians 1:31 tells us this way: *"...he that glorieth, let him glory in the Lord."* We should make a point to boast, glory, and brag in the Lord every chance we get. Boasting about the Lord to a humble Believer will quicken their Spirit and make them glad. Boasting in the Lord increases the hearer's faith ("So then faith cometh by hearing, and hearing by the word of God," Romans 10:17) and your own as well.

Blessing the Lord at all times helps us to magnify Him. When you magnify something, you make the thing bigger, easier to see or observe. When we magnify the Lord, we make Him bigger than our hardship or obstacles. When we magnify the Lord, we keep Him as Lord over our lives. We give Him the place of preeminence which belongs solely to Him. We don't magnify our problems, challenges, or obstacles. Indeed, we don't focus on them at all when we magnify the Lord because we make Him bigger than anything else in our lives.

Overcomers don't magnify the Lord alone. They can, but they prefer to invite others to magnify the Lord with them. Overcomers invite others to exalt His name with them. Often during praise and worship at church, I'll grab someone and dance with them because I want others to magnify Him and exalt Him with me.

I believe rejoicing in and praising the Lord are spiritual weapons. I believe Overcomers can use the garment of praise to combat the spirit of heaviness (see Isaiah 61:2), which I like to think of as depression. Keeping a praise on our lips helps us fight the enemy. Praise helps prevent us from falling into a spirit of depression (more on this in a later Key).

Paul picked up this same concept in Ephesians 5:20, *"Giving thanks always for all things unto God and the Father in the name of our Lord Jesus Christ."* He didn't tell us to give thanks only when things are going well. He said to give thanks ALWAYS for ALL things. This includes the good, the bad, and the ugly. If you're sick, give thanks. If you're lonely, give thanks. If you're having financial difficulties, give thanks. If you're facing persecution, give thanks. If you're having marital problems, give thanks. When you focus on the Lord, and His grace, mercy, forgiveness, deliverance, and salvation, you'll give thanks too.

Let me make something abundantly clear. I am by no means suggesting you bury your head in the sand, praising the Lord, and not taking care of your business. No! What I'm saying is I know you're facing problems. So am I. Everyone reading this book is facing problems. If you stay focused on the problems, you won't be able to praise the Lord until after He delivers you. However, if you stay focused on the Lord, you'll be able to bless Him at ALL times. I want you to bless God in everything you go through. You see, blessing Him at all times is indicative of spiritual maturity, as well as the strength of your faith. Let's talk about faith next.

## KEY 8 - LUKE 8:48

**"And He said unto her, 'Daughter be of good comfort: thy faith hath made thee whole, go in peace.'"**

Imagine struggling with an infirmity for twelve years. You've gone to doctors. You've prayed. You've tried the special diet well-meaning family and friends recommended. All to no avail. The illness won't go away. Perhaps you've resigned yourself to believing God doesn't want to heal you. Maybe you're angry with God. Why, oh why does He continue to let you suffer this way? You become angry, bitter, and cynical. Did God allow me to be born so I could suffer?

And then one day someone tells you about a man. Your friends and family tell you the man is in town and everyone is talking about Him. He can perform miracles. He's healing people. You decide to see Him. Maybe He can heal you as well.

## *Overcomer*

A throng of people crowd the man, and you can barely see Him. You didn't come all this way, get this close, only to go home disappointed. You decide to press your way through the crowd. Your determination is pushed by the belief, "If I could just touch His garment, I'll get my healing." Immediately, upon touching His garment, you receive your healing.

He turns around looking for the person who touched Him. You confess it was you and He says, "…thy faith hath made thee whole."

Our faith, our belief, in the Lord Jesus Christ can accomplish remarkable things. Our faith in Him saves, heals, and delivers us. Our faith rests in the power of God (1 Corinthians 2:5). Overcomers' faith believes Christ is who He says He is and He can, and will, accomplish what He says He will accomplish. Our faith gives us an inexplicable boldness. Our faith allows us to believe the unbelievable. And when we can believe God for the unbelievable, we become unstoppable, unshakeable, immoveable, always abounding in the work of the Lord (see 1 Corinthians 15:58).

As your car requires gasoline to drive, faith is the energy propelling us forward. Faith keeps us going. Faith sees what's hidden. Overcomers see victory over obstacles before the battle is won. Faith gives you boldness to declare you're healed in

Jesus' name when you've received a scary diagnosis and unknown prognosis. Faith will make you declare freedom over loved ones charged with crimes they didn't commit. Faith tells you to buy the furniture for the house before you go to closing. Faith in the power of God helps you forgive the person who doesn't show any remorse for what they've done to you. Faith empowers you to *"...love your enemies, bless them that curse you, do good to them that hate you, and pray for them which despitefully use you, and persecute you,"* (Matthew 5:44).

Walking as an Overcomer is impossible without faith because the Bible says pleasing God is impossible without faith (Hebrews 11:6). The scripture goes on to say, *"...for he that cometh to God must believe that He is, AND that He is a rewarder of them that diligently seek Him."* Let's take another look at the woman with the illness in the context of Hebrews 11:6.

Apparently, the woman believed the reports she'd heard about Jesus. She also believed He IS a rewarder. Believing in God and believing He's a rewarder is the true definition of faith. Faith believes God is going to reward. You see, belief IN God's existence isn't enough; demons believe and tremble (see James 2:19). You have to believe He is a rewarder to those who diligently seek Him.

## *Overcomer*

This woman diligently sought Christ. She didn't let the crowd discourage her. Some of us would have given up and returned home. I can see me now, "...Look at the line to get to him. Forget this. I'm leaving." I would have gone home and missed my blessing. The woman didn't let the crowd dissuade her. She pressed her way through. She stayed. She set her heart on being healed by Jesus, and she didn't let anything stop her. The woman was healed (cured) and made whole. The word "whole" means to save, deliver or protect; heal, preserve, do well, be whole[8]. This woman is an Overcomer. And you are an Overcomer too.

As an Overcomer, expect your faith to grow (see 2 Thessalonians 1:3). God wants you to believe Him for the miraculous. God wants you to expect Him to move on your behalf. Faith is a spiritual weapon which will press you into the presence of God where you will find joy and peace in the midst of trials. Your faith will help you praise the Lord amid sorrows. Your faith will help you see beyond what's right in front of you. Your faith will help you stay hopeful. Let's take a look at the role of hope in the life of the Overcomer.

---

[8] Strong's Numbers G4982

## KEY 9 - HEBREWS 11:1

**"Now faith is the substance of things hoped for, the evidence of things not seen."**

What exactly is hope? Romans 8:24 tells us *"...hope that is seen is not hope..."* As a noun, hope is the thing you're desiring. Hope is the result or the fruit of your prayers. You have faith in God for that which you're hoping.

Faith brings hope to life. Faith makes the thing hoped for real - before it manifests in your life. Overcomers ensure the thing they're hoping for aligns with God's word before they apply their faith. Once you are sure the thing you want aligns with God's word and begin praying and having faith, the Overcomer counts it as done.

Overcomers hold on to their hope, and if they feel their hope wavering, they go to the Lord in prayer asking for more strength. Yes, hope is instrumental to the Overcomer's ability to prevail over life's trials and tests.

## *Overcomer*

Unfortunately, one of Satan's primary tactics is attacking the believer's hope with doubt. If he can render you hopeless, you won't pray or apply faith to your situation. As an Overcomer, you cannot allow Satan to steal your hope. You must guard your hope; you must hold on to your hope. Maintaining your hope is a spiritual weapon enabling you to believe and trust God for the blessings He's promised you.

*"Who against hope believed in hope, that he might become the father of many nations, according to that which was spoken, 'So shall thy seed be',"* *(Romans 4:18).*

This verse in Romans 4 speaks about God's promise to Abraham in Genesis in which He tells Abraham he would become the father of many nations. When God spoke the promise to Abraham in Genesis 17:17, the Bible says *"...Abraham fell upon his face, and laughed..."* because he didn't believe he would have a son with his wife, Sarah. In due season, Sarah became pregnant in her old age and gave birth to the promised child, Isaac.

Regardless how the promise sounds, how far-fetched, believe and trust God. Follow His instructions. Obey His word. Hope for everything God promised you. If God told you you'd one day own a home, believe Him. If God said He would heal you then believe Him. If God told you your wayward children would become mighty men and women of God, believe Him. Stand fast in your hope, apply faith, pray, and believe God to bring the promise to pass in His timing.

I remember when I wanted to break into the information technology field. I didn't know much about computers or software. I used a computer for work, and I used my personal computer to write and surf the web. I hadn't taken any programming courses and didn't know anything about testing software or reading requirements. On the surface, my chances of becoming a software tester looked slim. I knew I needed a change and software testing sounded interesting.

I spoke to a few co-workers, seeking their advice about breaking into the field. Some people told me getting the job was impossible because I didn't have a college degree at the time. However, a few of them encouraged me and gave me excellent advice. I took my co-workers' advice, and when a position became available, I applied. One of my co-workers applied for the position as well. She'd previously applied but wasn't selected. In so many words she was told the next open position would be hers. She made sure to share this information with me and my faith staggered, but I had hope.

## *Overcomer*

In my spirit, I knew this was the job for me. And I was eventually offered the position. People couldn't believe I got the job because my co-worker had a technical background as well as more experience. I felt bad for her, but I was excited for myself at the same time.

You see, hope gives you confidence. Hope helped me anticipate and expect the job. My faith gave my hope substance *(...Now faith is the substance of things hoped for...)*. Overcomers don't let go of their hope. Overcomers keep hope alive. Overcomers know if the thing hoped for doesn't manifest, God has something better in store for them. So, they keep hoping.

Perhaps you're too afraid to hope for something due to past disappointments. I need you to let go of the past and its failures and press on. Don't let the enemy steal your hope or you're likely to become bitter and cynical like Naomi.

You remember the story in the book of Ruth. Naomi, her husband, and their two sons left Bethlehem because of a famine and moved to Moab. After they lived in that country awhile, her husband and both sons died. Naomi decided to move back to Bethlehem and her daughter-in-law, Ruth, decided to go with her.

## 25 Keys to Walking Victoriously

When Naomi returned to her country, she told the people not to call her Naomi (meaning my delight) but to call her Mara because *"...the Almighty hath dealt very bitterly with me. I went out full, and the Lord hath brought me home again empty: why then call ye me Naomi, seeing the Lord hath testified against me, and the Almighty hath afflicted me?"* (Ruth 1:20-21).

Since life had dealt harshly with her, Naomi didn't want to be referred to as "my delight" anymore. She related to bitter (Mara), and that label was her preference. When a person loses their hope, they gradually descend into a pit of blinded, bitter despair. They can't see with spiritual eyes. Naomi couldn't see the wonderful future which was in store for her lineage. She couldn't see God had a bigger plan. And so, it is with us.

We can't always see what God is doing. And that's fine! We don't need to always see what He's doing. We need to maintain our hope. Let me leave you with this final scripture:

*"Be of good courage, and He shall strengthen your heart, all ye that hope in the Lord," (Psalm 31:24).*

# Overcomer

## *KEY 10 - PHILIPPIANS 3:13*

**"Brethren, I count not myself to have apprehended: but this one thing I do, forgetting those things which are behind, and reaching forth unto those things which are before..."**

Let it go. Your past hurts, disappointments, rejections, and failures, as well as your past successes, wins, and victories. I'm sure telling you to forget your past successes, wins, and victories sound strange. Stick with me. I'll explain those in a minute. Let all of it go. Overcomers don't live in the past nor keep revisiting the past unless it's to strengthen someone with their testimony.

I dwelled in the past so much it hindered what God was presently trying to perform in my life. I was stuck on my previous disappointments. Life hadn't worked out for me the way I'd hoped, and I was angry and bitter. I stopped hoping and wouldn't trust God with my faith. I was miserable. I wanted and wished for many things but was too afraid to hope for and apply my faith for them. I was stuck.

You have to overcome your past. I've seen too many people unable to enjoy now because they can't get over their pasts. I've seen 40, and 50-year-old women stuck, unable to enjoy healthy relationships because of the past. I've seen grown women cry over their absent fathers and verbally abusive mothers. Their past hurts and disappointments have hindered these beautiful women from pressing into everything God has for them.

The past will rob you of your destiny if you let it. God has wonderful blessings in store for you, but your past will cause you to miss out. And trust me, you don't want to miss out on anything God has for you.

The past is a thief. The past is one of the biggest challenges I've had to overcome. I had to overcome my mom's death and the loneliness I felt afterward.

I am the youngest of my parents six children. When my mom died, my sister had a family, and my two oldest brothers had families. The two brothers closest in age to me (ten and seven years my senior) went into their own shells, dealing with the grief the best way they knew how. None of us were yet walking with the Lord. I felt like I had no one with whom I could

## *Overcomer*

share the pain of losing my son and my mother. I think I internalized my grief, building an impenetrable wall around myself. I was lonely inside my self-imposed prison but was afraid to allow anyone access. Loneliness became my roommate.

Eventually, the Lord sent me to a church where people chipped away at the wall I built around my heart. Tearing down the wall was difficult, but they did it. They showered me with love and affirmation. They included me in their lives and prayed for me. Although I was close to my biological family, my church family possessed something special or rather extraordinary. I had something in common with them: Jesus Christ. The love, patience, and acceptance I received from them helped heal me of the loneliness I felt for my mother. Remember, my mother passed away four months after I turned 18. I was a baby. If I wanted to press on to what God had in store for me, I had to release my mother, and the abandonment I felt after her death. As my grief healed, I was able to live life and enjoy the blessings God gave me.

I mentioned earlier that you also have to forget your past successes and victories. This sounds strange to me, so I know it sounds strange to you but let me explain what the Holy Spirit means.

## 25 Keys to Walking Victoriously

Have you ever met someone who's living in the glory days of their past? We've all seen these people: the former high school prom queen or the former high school football star. They graduated high school but have been reliving those same glory days for 30 years. Wait…. you mean to tell me you haven't accomplished anything else in 30 years? Apparently not and so they keep reliving the past.

Past successes and wins can hinder your future when you never stretch or challenge yourself to accomplish anything else. Yes, be excited about your wins. Be excited about your past accomplishments but know God has much, much more for you.

God's Overcomers use their pasts as springboards toward greater levels of anointing and blessing. God's Overcomers use their pasts to minister to others who are experiencing similar situations. Overcomers prevail over the hurts, disappointments, failures, successes, and wins of the past and are looking forward to future endeavors with zeal and anticipation.

Another way to overcome the past is to remember you are a new creature in Christ (2 Corinthians 5:17). The old things have passed away and *"…all things are become new."* All the old stuff is gone. God has newness awaiting you. God wants to use you in new ways. He wants to show and teach you a new way of living, of being. Again, staying stuck in the past will rob

## *Overcomer*

you of the new things God wants to give you and perform through you. Your past isn't worth missing the beauty of your present and your future. Stop letting what happened to you all those years ago control your life. Holding on to the hurt and pain isn't worth the agony you're experiencing now.

Overcome the past. Overcome disappointment. Overcome hurt. Remember the definition of overcome: subdue, conquer, overcome, prevail, get the victory[9]. You get the victory over your past when your past no longer rules you through your emotions, feelings, or actions.

Imagine how Paul felt when he reflected on his pre-Christ life. He remembered he persecuted the church, throwing men and women in jail. He remembered how Jesus challenged his unbelief on the road to Damascus. At the beginning of his ministry, he knew the other disciples doubted his conversion. Paul's past could have hindered his ministry work, but it didn't. He could have told Jesus he wasn't worthy to preach the Gospel. He could have let insecurity, regret, and shame render him ineffective, but he didn't.

---

[9] Strong's Numbers G3528

## 25 Keys to Walking Victoriously

Paul could have also walked in a spirit of pride because of his ancestry. Paul laid it all out for us: *"Circumcised the eighth day, of the stock of Israel, of the tribe of Benjamin, an Hebrew of the Hebrews; as touching the law, a Pharisee...,"* (Philippians 3:5). He summed up his lineage by saying, *"But what things were gain to me, those I counted loss for Christ...and do count them but dung, that I may win Christ..."* (Philippians 3:7-8b). Paul put his qualifications and lineage on the back burner and let the Lord use him. You see how our pasts can hinder us in multiple ways? We need to forget about it if the past is going to hinder our obedience to and work for the Lord Jesus Christ.

Don't allow your past to keep you stuck. Press beyond your past. Overcome it. Prevail over it. Offer your past up to the Lord and let Him use your experience as He sees fit. Use your past for God's glory, not your detriment.

*Overcomer*

## KEY 11 - MATTHEW 6:14

**"For if ye forgive men their trespasses, your heavenly Father will also forgive you."**

One of the quickest ways to release the past is through forgiveness. Believe it or not, forgiveness is one of my least favorite topics to teach in Bible study or my women's group. Everyone wants forgiveness from God and others, but many don't want to forgive. People expect others to forgive them, but they come up with excuses when they need to forgive someone else.

I firmly believe many people cannot move beyond their pasts because they refuse to forgive the trespasses committed against them. Perhaps feeling justified in withholding forgiveness is human nature, especially when you consider we believe trespasses committed against us are more heinous than those we committed against others and undeserving of forgiveness. Which isn't true.

I don't want to make light of what happened to you. I don't want to downplay the intensity of the abuse and hurts you've experienced. I know some things seem impossible to forgive. However, we must forgive. Let's take a look at the next verse:

> *"But if ye forgive not men their trespasses, neither will your Father forgive your trespasses," (Matthew 6:15).*

Trespass is defined as an unintentional error or willful transgression; fall, fault, offense, sin, trespass[10]. Whether the transgression against you was unintentional or willful, we are instructed to forgive. When we expect forgiveness from God for our trespasses but don't want to forgive others, we step into the place of God as judge. He's the righteous judge. We act as unrighteous judges (especially when it comes to trespasses against us and the pain we feel).

People mistakenly think forgiving others means we're condoning the offense. Forgiving someone doesn't mean you agree or excuse what they did. Forgiveness says we aren't expecting payment for the offense.

---

[10] Strong's Numbers G3900

## *Overcomer*

Forgiving someone shows the Lord we're willing to extend the grace to others He's extended to us. Forgiveness is steeped in love, obedience, grace, and mercy. Forgiveness shows the Lord we put His Word, His commands, before our feelings and emotions. Releasing others and the pain they've caused also show the Lord we trust Him.

Unforgiveness is bondage for the one refusing to forgive. How can we walk as Overcomers if we're in bondage to unforgiveness? Unforgiveness binds your hands and feet, as well as your mind and heart, in shackles. Unforgiveness has your mind and heart in shackles. Unforgiveness makes you a slave. The memory of the person and what they did can set you off. The memory can make you hate. The memory can make you wish harm upon the offender. If you are a Christian, these attitudes don't belong in your heart despite what happened to you.

Forgiveness frees us from bondage. Forgiveness helps us overcome the sting of the past. It helps us embrace our offender with the grace, mercy, and love God showed us when we were still in sin.

Let me make a quick distinction: I believe with all my heart we can forgive immediately. I don't believe forgiveness is a process. However, healing can be a process. Many people won't forgive because they still feel hurt over what happened in the past.

I struggled in my early years because my father wasn't in my life the way I desired. Although I saw him occasionally, we didn't have the relationship I wanted. I loved my daddy and daydreamed about him riding in on his white stallion and rescuing me from all the loneliness and rejection I was experiencing. He didn't show up as I hoped, so I spent years angry with him, wondering what was wrong with me that made my father stay away from me.

In 2000, I was attending a church, and the Pastor's wife asked me to lead a song for one of our church celebrations. I asked my father, brothers, and sister to attend for support as I was scared out of my mind. My father promised he would attend. I was sitting in the church when I saw two of my brothers and my sister walk in. I was super excited. I kept watching the door for my father. He never showed.

After the service ended, I asked my siblings about our dad, and one of my brothers told me our father called him to let me know he couldn't make the church service. I was devastated because he didn't show and because he didn't call me himself. I went home and, later in the evening, cried like a baby. I remember saying to the Lord I wanted my father to attend. I

## *Overcomer*

heard the Lord say, "But your Father was there." He was talking about Himself, and He was pleased with my obedience to sing. I sat on my bed in awe and was healed from that moment from my father's absence. I forgave him and moved on.

Years later, I invited my father to my college graduation, and although he didn't attend, I didn't get upset. I remember telling my siblings I didn't expect him to show up. You see, I realized I needed validation and acceptance from my earthly father but never received them. Since then I've pressed into my Heavenly Father, and I look to Him for validation, acceptance, and love, and I receive them every time.

Over the years, I've had to counsel other women who were going through the same anger and bitterness toward their fathers I experienced with my own. I could minister to them from a place of love because the Lord healed me. The unforgiveness toward my father was gone, and his absence no longer controlled me, my emotions, or my actions. I can honestly say I love, honor, and respect my father and want God's best for him. He's a great man with an uncanny sense of humor, and I bless God for his life.

Joseph is an excellent example of forgiveness. His brothers sold him into slavery. He was betrayed, separated from his family, and thrown in an Egyptian prison. If anyone had the right to hold unforgiveness in his heart, it was Joseph. Genesis 50:19-20 records Joseph telling his brothers, *"...Fear not: for am I in the place of God? But as for you, ye thought evil against me; but God meant it unto good, to bring to pass, as it is this day, to save much people alive."* Joseph recognized God's hand in his brothers' actions against him. He understood that although his brothers betrayed Him, God was in control of everything that happened to him.

Can we get to this place as well? Can we get to the place where we forgive people because we know God is ultimately in control? Can we answer, *"...am I in the place of God,"* with a resounding no? Let us stop trying to play God in others' lives - but want only God to be God in ours.

Free yourself from the bondage of unforgiveness and walk in freedom. Overcomers may find forgiving others difficult, but they extend forgiveness anyway because they refuse to let anything interfere with their relationships with God. They will forgive, heal, and forgive again if necessary. They prevail over and conquer unforgiveness so they can walk in liberty. If you're harboring unforgiveness, I urge you to forgive quickly and let God give you the victory.

# *Overcomer*

## *KEY 12 - ROMANS 12:2*

**"And be not conformed to this world: but be ye transformed by the renewing of your mind, that ye may prove what is that good, and acceptable, and perfect, will of God."**

Any discussion about walking as an Overcomer which fails to include Romans 12:2 is lacking because Christ constantly renews our mind. A changed mind enables us to walk as an Overcomer. Before we came to Christ, our ways of thinking were contrary to Christ's way of thinking. Our thinking contradicted His in many ways. If we keep those ways of thinking, we will never enjoy the Overcomer's victory.

Romans 12:2 admonishes us to be transformed. I love the term transformed because it brings to mind the process through which a caterpillar becomes a butterfly. Before transforming, the caterpillar sees the world through the eyes of a caterpillar. He's slow, crawling around on his belly. He has no concept of being able to fly. Oh, he has seen others transform. He's seen other animals fly, but he has never experienced flying for himself. Sprouting wings and flying around the backyard was inconceivable to the caterpillar.

Perhaps there's a knowing within him telling him he's destined for greater. Maybe he knows the ability to fly is within him, but since crawling on his belly is his relegation, and crawling is all he knows, crawling is all he does.

People who don't know they're overcomers are like caterpillars. They've lived a certain way all their lives. They've struggled all their lives, allowing people to use them, being a victim, enduring abuse, suffering from depression, or addiction. They can't fathom a better life. Or perhaps they can, but they don't know how to attain it. They may not understand the significance of Christ coming to give them the abundant life (see John 10:10) and so they never strive to overcome, to conquer, prevail, to gain the victory. They're resigned to being the victim, to living beneath the blessings which are theirs in Christ Jesus. And forget about having peace and joy in the midst of a storm. They've never seen anyone endure a storm with peace or joy and can't believe doing so is possible. No matter how much you try to help them, they never transform because they can't or

## *Overcomer*

won't renew their minds. They don't realize they already possess the ability to sprout wings and fly.

Overcomers, on the other hand, start out like the caterpillar. They endure tough times with God's grace and mercy. Something triggers in the heart of the Overcomer when someone tells them they don't have to crawl around on their belly because God has a better way for them. The Overcomer hears the word of God and embraces it. Embracing it may take time but eventually, the Overcomer grasps the word, applies it to their lives, begins to renew their mind, and eventually sees a transformation. They know God has more for them and they purpose in their hearts to align their minds with biblical thinking.

The word renewing in Romans 12:2 includes the word "renovation" as one of its definitions. Some years ago, I taught a Bible series on "renewing" using the renovation of a home as an example. A few carpenters were in attendance in my bible class who helped me instruct by explaining the work that goes into renovating a home. I remember asking one of the young men if installing new appliances into an old home by simply plugging them in was possible. He explained new appliances require the installation of a new electrical system as it is unlikely the old system would be able to handle the new appliances. We also went into tearing up floors, installing new bathrooms, a new furnace, as well as the work needed in the basement and the attic. The detailed overview was presented as a spiritual correlation and blessed everyone in the class.

When we discuss renewing the mind, think about a renovation project. When God renews your mind through the word of God, you are undergoing a renovation project. Renovation projects require time, money, energy, and effort. Your spiritual renovation is going to cost you time, money, and energy as well. The beauty of this project is Christ already paid the price on your behalf. The only requirement is you go through the process.

If you're tired of suffering through every trial or test, never gaining or seeing victory or experiencing joy and peace, then allow the Holy Spirit to renew your mind. This renewal is of utmost importance. He wants to renew your mind so your transformation is apparent to all those who see or meet you. Overcomers are full of testimonies of how God transformed them by changing or renewing their minds. Overcomers are quick to tell people about how God delivered them from defeatist thinking and mindsets.

Although Overcomers have been transformed, they understand transforming the mind is a life-long process. The

## *Overcomer*

more we study the Bible and apply its teachings to our lives, the more transformation we will see. We will grow and mature in our walks with Christ and people will be able to see the light because it will illuminate brighter with each passing day. You are an Overcomer. Let the Lord transform you into the beautiful woman of God He destined you to become.

## KEY 13 - 1 CORINTHIANS 15:10

**"But by the grace of God I am what I am: and His grace which [was bestowed] upon me was not in vain; but I labored more abundantly than they all: yet not I, but the grace of God which was with me."**

Who are you? No, not your name.

Who ARE you?

One of the biggest problems I've seen since coming to Christ is folks not knowing who they are. They haven't yet found their identity in Christ. They strive for titles thinking the title will validate them, but they're left feeling empty.

When I ask who you are, I'm asking you who are you IN Christ. Many people don't know. And an Overcomer who doesn't know who she is in Christ is an easy target for the enemy. He will have you chasing your tail and chasing anybody you feel can tell you who you are. If someone tells you - you're a teacher, you'll believe them and ask the pastor when you can have an opportunity to teach. If someone tells you - you're a pastor, you'll grab ahold of the calling and try to pastor a church. If someone tells you - you're a prophet, you'll run around trying to prophesy to everyone, giving them a "word" God never instructed you to give them. KNOWING who you are in Christ stops the rat race.

Knowing who you are in Christ empowers you to state with full assurance, *"But by the grace of God I am what I am..."* No devil in hell can sway the person who knows who she is in Christ. Although the Apostle Paul is sharing his journey in becoming an apostle with us in this, and the surrounding verses, my question to you is deeper than knowing your title. You see, Paul understood, *"...whom He did predestinate, them He also called: and whom He called, them He also justified: and whom he justified, them he also glorified,"* (Romans 8:30). Paul understood who he was in Christ and where he stood in Christ.

Paul didn't miraculously forget he persecuted the church of Jesus Christ. He didn't forget he had men and women dragged off to prison. He didn't forget he harassed the early Christians. He didn't forget he was in the audience when

Stephen suffered death by stoning. Paul remembered but he knew Jesus called him as an apostle.

Overcomers remember how they used to behave. Overcomers acknowledge their current temptations and failures. However, Overcomers don't fall into condemnation because they understand they are called, justified, and glorified. Overcomers know there's a call on their lives as Paul did. Overcomers know they are more than conquerors (Romans 8:37). You need to know as well.

If you don't know or understand who you are in Christ, you'll continue apologizing for the mistakes you made in your past. You will never feel worthy to be in a relationship with a holy God. You'll never forgive yourself, and you'll keep beating yourself up for past sins. You may get caught in what I call the vicious works cycle. The work's cycle is when Christians try to "pay" God for His grace by performing as many works as they can for Him. We should work for the Lord because we love Him, not because we're trying to earn His love or repay Him for His grace and mercy.

Yes, knowing who we are and what we've received through Christ's sacrifice on the cross will help all of us walk as Overcomers. Knowing who we are should fill us with humility and help us extend grace and mercy to a dark and dying world as God extended them to us through His Son.

As you grow in the knowledge of who you are in Christ, you will eventually be able to say, "I am what I am," despite what others think or say about you. About nine years ago, I had to deal with someone spreading rumors about me, going as far as lying about me to my Pastor. I respected this person, and their words caused me to doubt who I was in Christ and what I'd been called to perform in the kingdom of God.

The Lord didn't allow me to wallow in self-doubt for long though. He soon talked with me, affirming and confirming for me who I was in Him as well as what He'd called me to perform in the kingdom. Since then, I've never doubted I am a teacher of the gospel. I am what I am, despite what anyone thinks, says, or believes about me.

Since I am what I am, I don't strive to prove who I am to anyone nor try to be the best Bible teacher. I want to be an anointed Bible teacher. Endeavoring to be the best at anything is breeding ground for competition and jealousy, and I refuse to succumb to those spirits.

I've learned God graces us to be what He called us to be, but each of us will operate in our anointing differently. My cousin is a Bible teacher who gets inspiration for Bible lessons from landscaping. One of my friends is a Bible teacher who gets inspiration from Disney movies and Dr. Seuss books (you should hear her lesson on "Horton Hears a Who"). I tend to get ideas for Bible lessons from books, movies, tv shows, everyday life, everywhere. I look for lessons in everything.

Overcomers have stopped comparing their gifting or calling to anyone else's. They've learned comparison isn't worth the frustration. Overcomers are comfortable and confident in who Christ created them to be. When you're comfortable and confident, you won't need to prove yourself to anyone nor will you compete with anyone.

Say it with me, "I am what I am!"

*Overcomer*

## KEY 14 - ROMANS 8:14

**"For as many as are led by the Spirit of God, they are the sons of God."**

Who, or what, leads you through life? Are you more led by success, money, or emotions, than by the Lord? Be honest.

I want to discuss in this chapter the dangers of being led by our emotions. Our emotions are real. Some of the emotions or feelings we experience include fear, anger, sadness, joy, disgust, anxiety, shame, confusion, embarrassment, envy, frustration, happiness, insecurity, loneliness, love, pride, relief, suspicion, terror, and worry. The list is more extensive than what I've included, but I think you get the point.

Unfortunately, some of us live our lives based on what we're feeling. For example, how often have you not praised the Lord, gone to church, or exercised because of how you felt? How many times have you called in sick to work because you didn't want to deal with a co-worker, boss, or client? How many times have you felt down about yourself because you didn't "feel" pretty or sexy or confident?

Experiencing emotions is normal and healthy. Being led by them is not. The quickest way to live life on a roller coaster is living according to your emotions. Your emotions can become a little "g" god. If your emotions tell you to go, you'll go. If your emotions tell you to stop, you'll stop. If your emotions tell you to view someone with suspicion, you'll view them with suspicion. How can we overcome our emotions and stop walking according to them?

> *"For as many as are led by the Spirit of God, they are the sons of God," (Romans 8:14).*

Christians should be led only by the Spirit of God. The Spirit of God will never deceive nor harm us. If you want to walk as an Overcomer, let God's Spirit lead you.

The word "led" in Romans 8:14 includes "induce" as one of its definitions[11]. According to Webster's, induce means to move by persuasion or influence; to call forth or bring about by influence or stimulation.[12] When our emotions and feelings

---

[11] Strong's Numbers G70
[12] https://www.merriam-webster.com/dictionary/induce

## *Overcomer*

influence us to act, we can find ourselves in trouble. Think about people who are in jail because their feelings led them to commit a crime against someone. Also, think about people who married without heeding wisdom. Wisdom cried out, but they were following their emotions and didn't heed the wisdom they heard. You see, feelings and emotions can cause us to make unwise decisions.

The Spirit of the Lord is all-knowing (omniscient) and all-powerful (omnipotent). He knows the consequences of the decisions we're making and either encourages or discourages our decisions based upon His will for our lives. Unfortunately, when our feelings and emotions lead and influence our decisions, we'll make unwise or hasty decisions leading to hardship.

Let's talk about ten people who were led by their emotions in Numbers 13. In this story, Moses sent twelve men to spy out Canaan. The twelve men saw the same thing - a land flowing with milk and honey. They brought back samples of the land. However, ten of them were discouraged by the Amalekites, Hittites, Jebusites, and Amorites dwelling in the land. Two of them, Joshua and Caleb, were not moved by the inhabitants. Unlike the fearful ten, they were not afraid. On the contrary, Caleb told the people although all those enemies lived in the land, the children of Israel were able to possess the land, *"...for we are well able to overcome it,"* (Numbers 13:30).

The ten didn't want to hear what Caleb said. Instead, they continued to discourage the children of Israel saying, *"The land through which we have gone to search it, is a land that eateth up the inhabitants thereof; and all the people that we saw in it are men of a great stature,"* (Numbers 13:32).

The ten men were afraid of the people in the land, and their fear caused them to discourage everyone around them. They discouraged the children of Israel so badly the Bible says the people cried and turned against Moses and Aaron. Moreover, the ten men became so discouraged by what they saw, that they viewed themselves as powerless and insignificant.

> *"And there we saw the giants, the sons of Anak, which come of the giants: and we were in our own sight as grasshoppers, and so we were in their sight,"*
> *(Numbers 13:33).*

Where did that thought and imagination originate? It certainly didn't come from God. Since they saw themselves as grasshoppers, they thought the inhabitants of the land felt the same way about them and how they felt stopped them in their tracks. They refused to heed Caleb's advice to take the land.

## *Overcomer*

You see how feelings led them to discourage others? How are your feelings causing you to behave? How are your feelings inducing you to lead others?

Let's take a look at what Joshua and Caleb said in response to the people:

*"...the land, which we passed through to search it, is an exceeding good land. If the Lord delight in us, then He will bring us into this land, and give it us; a land which floweth with milk and honey. Only rebel not ye against the Lord, neither fear ye the people of the land; for they are bread for us: their defense is departed from them, and the Lord is with us: fear them not," (Numbers 14:7-9).*

The people were in rebellion because God already promised to give Canaan to them, but they refused to claim the land by faith. God promised to give some blessings to you and me as well but, if we're not careful, our feelings and emotions will cause us to rebel against God and miss those blessings.

Joshua and Caleb were Overcomers. They were ready to go in and take the land, but the doubters ruined the opportunity for everyone. The ten doubters provoked the Lord and Moses had to come to their defense.

## 25 Keys to Walking Victoriously

*"...how long will it be ere they believe me, for all the signs which I have shewed among them? I will smite them with the pestilence, and disinherit them, and will make of thee a greater nation and mightier than they," (Numbers 14:11-12).*

Overcomers have the Holy Spirit abiding in them, and He will lead and guide us into all truth. We must submit to His will and trust Him irrespective of how the situation looks or how we feel. I know some of the obstacles you're facing seem insurmountable. I know they seem impossible. God does some of His best work in the impossible. And that's what He was saying about the children of Israel in verse 11. He was reminding them about all the signs and wonders He already performed on their behalf. Now think back.

Think about all the challenges you've already overcome. Think about how God came through for you before. He delivered you then; He'll deliver you again. Overcomers never forget the power of God. Make sure you don't either.

When negative feelings arise, speaking to you, frightening and hindering you, purpose in your heart you won't allow your feelings to block your blessings. Set your heart to obey God at any cost. When you are facing giants, remind yourself God is bigger, mightier, and stronger than those giants, and has your back. Go into the land and possess what God has ordained for you to possess.

## KEY 15 - PHILIPPIANS 4:6-7

**"Be anxious for nothing, but in everything by prayer and supplication with thanksgiving let your requests be made known to God. And the peace of God, which surpasses all comprehension, will guard your hearts and your minds in Christ Jesus," (NASB).**

I sat in Starbucks the day before my first chemo infusion sipping a Caramel Macchiato. My thoughts and emotions were all over the place. The oncologist told my husband and me some people have adverse effects from chemotherapy, but the nurses would administer the proper pre-meds to lower my chances of having an allergic reaction. I was petrified. I wanted to have faith God would bring me out with a strong right hand, but I was also afraid I would die. If being afraid of cancer killing me wasn't enough, I had to be afraid of the chemotherapy killing me too. I desperately needed a Word from the Lord.

## *Overcomer*

I'm a worrier by nature. I worry enough for you, me, and everyone else. I was worried whether I would live or die. I was worried about my nine-year-old daughter and what would happen to her should I die. I worried if my husband would remarry and allow our daughter to call another woman, "Mommy". I worried about my 22-year-old son and my two-month-old granddaughter. I worried about my church. I worried about my extended family. I'm extremely close to many of my nieces and nephews and worried how my death would affect them. I wondered the same thing about my siblings.

As I sat in Starbucks, the Lord told me through Philippians 4:6-8 not to worry nor be anxious about the infusion I was facing the next day. He told me to bring everything to Him in prayer. He reassured me that as He had me in the palm of His hands, He also had my daughter, my son, my husband, my nieces and nephews, my siblings, and my church family.

The Lord reminded me to pray with thanksgiving. I had to dig deep to find the thanksgiving during my cancer treatments. The Lord reminded me to make ALL my requests to Him. I needed to get the worry and anxiety out of my heart, out of my soul, out of my mind, out of my spirit. I needed to trust Him with everything.

## 25 Keys to Walking Victoriously

As I cast my cares about the cancer treatments on Him, the peace which surpasses all understanding or comprehension guarded my heart and mind. As I reflect on the months I went through treatments, the amount of joy and peace I had are mind-boggling. I took selfies while sitting in the cancer infusion room. I brought my work laptop and worked during my treatments, participating in conference calls and completing various work-related tasks. I laughed during the Kelly and Michael Show and talked back to the television during the Wendy Williams Show (those two television shows entertained me during those long infusion appointments). And like I said earlier, I continued to sing on the praise team and teach my women's group at the church.

Many people didn't understand why I continued to work. I persevered at work, at home, and at church because the Lord told me to. I guess some people want to stop working, but some people need to stay active. Staying active helped keep my mind off the chemo's possible side effects as the drugs flowed through my veins. Staying active gave me something to think about other than the fact I was a cancer patient.

Philippians 4:8 teaches us what to think. Overcomers don't constantly think about what they're going through. They know

*Overcomer*

if they only think and worry about their problems they'll become depressed and more anxious.

Regardless what you're going through right now, I need you to focus on Philippians 4:6-8. I need you to stop being anxious. I need you to stop worrying. I also need you to lift everything up to the Lord in prayer, believing He hears you and is going to take care of you.

Remember to keep a heart of thanksgiving as you lift everything up to God in prayer. Learn to give thanks to Him for everything. When your mind is bombarded with negative thoughts, replace those thoughts with the things listed in Philippians 4:8. Choose to meditate on what's true, honest, just, pure, lovely, of good report, virtuous, and praiseworthy. Thinking on the things Paul instructs us to think on in Philippians 4:8 will increase and strengthen your faith. Speak those things aloud into the atmosphere. And be on guard against anyone who brings you negativity.

A special note: Soon after my breast cancer diagnosis, I called one of my cousins because she is a doctor and I wanted her professional opinion. I told her what the doctor said, and she gave me one of the best pieces of advice I received during my cancer journey. She said, "Aretha, stay away from negative people. Studies have shown that people who have a strong support system, speaking encouraging words to them, fare better than those who don't have a support system or those who are surrounded by negative people."

When I told my husband what my cousin said, we decided we wouldn't tell specific people about my cancer diagnosis, primarily because they are negative and would probably say something discouraging to my husband, our kids, or to me.

I believe heeding my cousin's advice, along with standing on the scriptures the Lord gave me, saved my life. I shared this story with you because I wanted to show you how important our attitudes and thoughts are in our journeys in being Overcomers.

As you change your lifestyle to walking as an Overcomer, people aren't going to be excited for you. Those people will try to remind you of your past, your failures, your mess ups, what you used to do, and how you used to behave. I need you to run for your life away from them until you grow stronger in the faith. Please don't allow Negative Nancy to hinder your blessing from the Lord. Keep your mind on Him and let Him deliver you.

*Overcomer*

## KEY 16 - ISAIAH 26:3

**"Thou wilt keep him in perfect peace, whose mind is stayed on thee: because he trusteth in thee."**

Let's talk about peace a little more, shall we? We know the enemy comes to kill, steal, and destroy (John 10:10). One of the things he attacks is our peace because praising, worshiping, and serving the Lord, and loving His people are difficult without peace. The enemy is well aware of this. He attacks our peace to keep us in a constant state of chaos and confusion. Where chaos and confusion abide, you will not find the Holy Spirit. He does not dwell in such environments.

Satan is the author of confusion, and he spreads his poison everywhere. Confusion breeds chaos. They go hand-in-hand. When you find peace, you find tranquility. Peace in Isaiah 26:3 is defined as, safe, well, happy, welfare, health, prosperity, rest, safety, be well. This is God's will for us.

## 25 Keys to Walking Victoriously

Notice the verse says God will keep those in perfect peace whose minds are stayed on Him. If we allow the enemy to steal our focus and our minds from God's peace and place them on the confusion and chaos around us, living in the perfect peace God promises in Isaiah 26:3 will be impossible.

The wording in this chapter reminds me of what we discussed in Philippians 4:8 where Paul tells us which things to think on:

> *"Finally, brethren, whatever is true, whatever is honorable, whatever right, whatever is pure, whatever is lovely, whatever is of good repute, if there is any excellence and if anything worthy of praise, dwell on these things,"*
> *(NASB).*

When we keep our minds on God, these are the things we'll think about, and Satan hates when we think on the good. Satan doesn't want us to meditate or think about positive, encouraging, or godly things. He wants us to think on the opposite. He wants us to think about what's corrupt, defiled, immoral, impure, disagreeable, unworthy, unimportant, or shameful. Yet, those words don't edify, comfort, nor bless.

Satan wants nothing more than to steal your peace and he will use whatever tool is available to bring about his desired results. Satan will use your loved ones, your job, and even your church. The enemy will cause financial and health problems to steal your peace. He will use anything or anybody made available to him to make us anxious, discontent, and confused. We have to battle against him if we desire to walk as Overcomers in Christ.

You have to guard your peace, notwithstanding what's going on in your life. Remember in Philippians 4:7 the Bible said the peace of God will guard, or keep, your hearts and minds through Christ Jesus? Peace guards our hearts (seat of our emotions) and minds (seat of our intelligence and reasoning). Therefore, we need to protect our peace so it can guard our hearts and minds and the emotions and intellect arising from them.

One of the best ways to guard your peace is staying focused on God. I cannot emphasize this enough. Allow my transparency once again as I refer to my breast cancer journey. Within two weeks of being diagnosed, I'd seen more doctors than I'd seen in my entire life. I learned words I never thought I'd have to know. I was experiencing emotions I never thought I'd have to experience. I was disturbed and distraught. I was confused and felt like I was living in a fugue. If I wasn't scheduled for one appointment, I was scheduled for another. If

I wasn't on the phone with one doctor's office, it was another. I was quickly growing weary.

Please keep in mind, everyone I knew who'd received a cancer diagnosis was dead except my brother and brother-in-law who both received their cancer diagnoses during the same year of my journey (they passed away December 2014 and December 2015 respectively). I honestly believed everyone diagnosed with cancer died. I was beyond stressed out. I was beyond confused, thinking:

"How did this happen to me?"

"Why did this happen to me?"

"Why was I the 1-out-of-8 women diagnosed?"

When I went to sleep, cancer was on my mind. I dreamed about cancer. I woke up with cancer on my mind. I was driving myself crazy.

I had to get to a place where I thought about God more than I thought about cancer. I started reading my Bible more. I started praying more. The more I sought Him, the more He revealed Himself to me. I want to encourage you to seek Him more.

I know life is difficult right now. I know you're wondering how you're going to endure. I know you're hurt, stressed out, and confused. It's ok. It really is. Go through the emotions but don't stay in that emotional place.

## *Overcomer*

Dear Overcomer - I want you to keep your mind "stayed" on God. Stayed means to prop, to lean upon or take hold of; to bear up; lay, lean, lie hard, rest self, stand fast, and sustain. We need to train our minds to stay on God and lean upon the Lord. We need to rest in Christ. We need to stand fast and let the Holy Spirit sustain us.

When we take our minds off the Lord, we go back to Proverbs 3:5 and resort to leaning to our own understanding. When we keep our minds on Him, He gives us clarity, comfort, and strength. When we keep our minds on Him, peace is our reward. Although confusion, chaos and every wicked thing imaginable is going on around us, we walk in joy, peace, and bold confidence toward the Lord.

Let me make one last point about peace. Peace is a fruit of the Holy Spirit:

> *"But the fruit of the Spirit is love, joy, peace, longsuffering, gentleness, goodness, faith, meekness, temperance…," (Galatians 5:22).*

We are given peace when the Holy Spirit comes to dwell inside us at the moment of salvation. Your peace is a gift from

God. Why on earth would you allow someone to steal from you what the Lord has gifted to you?

Handing our peace over to the enemy reminds me of people who like to re-gift birthday and Christmas presents. It would hurt my feelings if the gift I gave to one of my children was subsequently given to someone else. Let's say I bought one of my children a pair of shoes they desperately wanted. I present the shoes to my kid, they say thank you and appear happy. Three days later I see one of their friends wearing the shoes I gave them. Imagine how I'd feel. Imagine how you'd feel. Worst yet, imagine someone stealing the shoes from my child. I'd be more upset.

Similarly, why are we giving away our peace? Why let Satan steal the gift Christ died on the cross to gift to us? Satan doesn't have peace, and he doesn't want us to have peace either. Hence, he tries to steal it from us. Unfortunately, many of us let him have our peace without much of a fight.

Saints, we have to fight to maintain our peace. Overcomers can't permit distractions or diversions to bring chaos and confusion into their lives. Overcomers can't allow confusion and chaos to reign in their lives, destroying their peace. Overcomers can't settle for lives without peace. You need peace, and you deserve it. Hold on to it. Protect it. Guard it.

# Overcomer

## *KEY 17 - ISAIAH 54:17*

**"No weapon that is formed against thee shall prosper; and every tongue that shall rise against thee in judgment thou shalt condemn. This is the heritage of the servants of the Lord, and their righteousness is of me, saith the Lord."**

Weapons are going to form against you. Make no mistake about it. However, the Bible promises those weapons will NOT prosper; they will not succeed. You may get hit by a few of the weapons, they may sting, but they will not kill you, steal from you, nor destroy you (see John 10:10). You have an awesome God who protects you day and night. He doesn't sleep. He doesn't slumber.

What are these weapons forming against us? Any and everything. Weapons can include lies, gossip, illness, financial problems, or verbal or physical abuse. Weapons are anything which shakes your faith in God and makes you question His existence, His power, or His love for you.

## 25 Keys to Walking Victoriously

Overcomers don't run because of the weapons. Overcomers instead pick up spiritual weapons remembering those weapons are not carnal, "but mighty through God," (2 Corinthians 10:4). Overcomers dress themselves with the full armor (Ephesians 6:12-18).

By the time I became serious about Christian living, I was a mess from all the poor choices I'd made. I was depressed, angry, overwhelmed, confused, divorced, bankrupt, and enjoying my pity party, thank you very much. I didn't have any friends because I didn't like myself and didn't know how to be a friend. I was alone and lonely. I couldn't believe God could love someone like me.

Yes, God had a mess to contend with when I finally said "Yes, Lord" in 1997. He faced the mess named Aretha with grace, mercy, patience, and love, and He won me over. I still don't cross every "t" nor dot every "i", but I'm certainly better today than I was in August 1997 when I earnestly started seeking Him.

The Lord started teaching me about spiritual weapons to combat the enemy of my soul. I learned about those weapons, and I learned how to use them to fight back. I cannot conduct an exhaustive study in this chapter of those weapons (perhaps I'll write a book on this topic later), but I want to highlight a few of the weapons Overcomers use to gain the victory over the enemy.

**Faith**

Faith used to confuse me. I didn't understand it. I heard people say they had faith and bought a house, or got a car, a spouse, a new job, but those examples seemed shallow to me. Certainly, faith was more than the vehicle through which people obtained material blessings from God.

My answer came while reading 1 Corinthians 2:5, *"That your faith should not stand in the wisdom of men, but in the power of God."* Ohhhhhh - Ok - I gotcha now! My faith needed to be in God's POWER. I understood God is all-powerful, all-seeing, all-knowing. I understood God is omnipotent, omnipresent, and omniscient. I believed God parted the Red Sea. I believed God kept Daniel in the lion's den. I believed David killed Goliath with a stone. I believed God raised Lazarus from the dead. I believed Jesus was crucified, died, buried, resurrected, ascended on high, and sat at the right hand of the Father making intercession for me. I believed God's miraculous power. I needed to believe He is as powerful today, in my situation, as He was when He performed all the miracles we read about in the Bible. Since He had the power to perform those miracles before, He had the same power to perform similar miracles for me today.

I had to make it personal. You should personalize your faith too. Believe God will come through for you in His time and in His way. Believe you will spend eternity with the Lord. Believe you have boldness and confidence in the Lord and that you no longer have to be afraid of the enemy. Believe the Greater One lives in you (1 John 4:4). State boldly, "…if God be for us, who can be against us?" (Romans 8:31).

This type of faith is unshakeable. We may sway when hard times come, but the enemy is unable to uproot us because our foundation in God is sure. Use your faith to overcome the schemes of the devil.

**Prayer**

Prayer has been a staple throughout every section in this book thus far. I want to make something abundantly clear: Prayer is ESSENTIAL to a Christian's life. Prayer, at the most basic, is communication WITH God. Prayer isn't only monologue of you talking to God. Prayer is a dialogue. You talk to God, and He listens to you. He talks to you, and you listen to Him. Overcomers understand they are in a spiritual battle and they need to hear from the Commander-in-Chief (God). They

*Overcomer*

recognize the enemy is crafty and sneaky and only God knows how to overcome him. If we want to win the battles we're facing, we need to pray without ceasing.

**Fasting**

Jesus told His disciples certain things only come through prayer AND fasting (see Mark 9:29). Christians pray, but are we fasting as often as we should? One of the reasons we may not be seeing the victories we desire to see and are praying about could be because we aren't fasting.

Fasting means fasting from food. I have come across too many people who are fasting from television and Facebook. Fasting from extracurricular activities is wonderful but while you're fasting from them, make sure you're fasting from food specifically.

Please note, if you have a medical condition affected by fasting from food, please see your medical doctor before undergoing any fasts.

**The Bible**

After Jesus was baptized, He was led by the Spirit into the wilderness to be tempted by Satan for 40 days. In each instance in which Satan spoke to Him, the Bible records Jesus' response as being something previously written (see Matthew 4 and Luke 4). Jesus always replied, "It is written...". Since Jesus is our example, we should respond to the enemy the same way. If the Word made flesh responded with the Word, shouldn't we respond in the same manner?

Knowing the Bible, speaking God's Word, and applying its instructions to the various situations you encounter in your walk with Christ are of utmost importance. Overcomers are students of the Bible and know to wield the sword of the Spirit (the Word of God) to combat the enemy's lies and temptations.

**Fellowship**

Fellowship with other Spirit-filled, Spirit-led believers is another weapon in our arsenal. When we're facing trials, tests, and temptations, we often stop coming to church. We'd much rather stay at home having our pity parties. However, fellowship with other Christians will encourage you and give you the wisdom you need to persevere. Isolating yourself or cutting off Word-filled people is a mistake. These individuals have the ability and desire to help you overcome the wiles of the devil. I urge you to reach out to your church's leadership team and ask for help. I encourage you to make friends with those who are

## *Overcomer*

chasing after God. *"Not forsaking the assembling of ourselves together, as the manner of some is; but exhorting one another: and so much the more, as ye see the day approaching,"* (Hebrews 10:25).

As the day of Jesus' return approaches, and it's approaching quickly, we need to fellowship with other Believers so we can exhort one another to stand in faith. We need to encourage others, and we need to be encouraged as well.

What are you going through today, dear Overcomer? Which weapons are being formed against you? Stand with your shield of faith ready to quench every single one of the enemy's fiery darts. You are an Overcomer, ready, willing, and able to win the battle waging against you.

## KEY 18 - EPHESIANS 6:12

**"For we wrestle not against flesh and blood, but against principalities, against powers, against rulers of the darkness of this world, against spiritual wickedness in high places."**

Since becoming a Christian, I've encountered a few battles with people. When I was younger in Christ and didn't know any better, I would pray against those individuals. I remember praying God would bind them up (I didn't know much, so don't judge me). Since those days, I've learned God doesn't want me to pray AGAINST people, especially other believers. He wants me to pray FOR them.

There was a particular person who treated me poorly for no apparent reason. Multiple people told me the degrading things she spoke against me. Although the words hurt, I tried my hardest not to retaliate or respond in anger. Her dislike hurt me because I looked up to her and genuinely liked her. My flesh wanted to hurt her as badly as she was hurting me but my spirit wouldn't allow me to do so. Instead, I prayed and trusted God, and the Lord vindicated me in due season.

I was perplexed because both of us were professing Christians. I didn't understand how two Holy Ghost filled people could treat one another so poorly. I was devastated and heartbroken. I went to the Lord in prayer, and I was encouraged by His response.

He led me to Ephesians 6:12 and told me to stop wrestling with the woman. He told me her opinions and approval weren't worth the stress I was experiencing. He gave me insight regarding her, and I started viewing her through God's eyes, soon realizing she needed love. She was being used by the enemy to sow discord among brethren (see Proverbs 6:19). And so, I prayed FOR her but AGAINST the demonic influence over her life. And I'm still praying!

I don't hold any animosity toward her. And whenever people start telling me what she's said about me, I stop them because her words don't mean anything to me anymore. I tell folks to pray for her instead of helping to spread poison.

This verse in Ephesians 6 helped me overcome the rejection and embarrassment I endured. My battle isn't against her. My battle is against the spirits speaking to and through her.

Thus, I don't focus on the flesh and blood because I'm not waging war against flesh and blood. I understand the spiritual battle, so I pray she is made free and whole.

My experience gave me a better understanding of the battle David endured with King Saul. When David and Saul returned from killing the Philistines,

> "...the women came out of the cities of Israel, singing and dancing, to meet king Saul, with tabrets, with joy, and with instruments of music. And the women answered one another as they played, and said, 'Saul hath slain his thousands, and David his ten thousands.' And Saul was very wroth, and the saying displeased him...and Saul eyed David from that day and forward," (1 Samuel 18:6-9).

The Bible records multiple instances in which Saul tried to kill David because of envy. However, David wouldn't touch Saul. David respected and loved Saul regardless what Saul did to him.

When we are under spiritual attack, we need to look to David's response to Saul as an example. We do not wrestle against flesh and blood. Our battle isn't with the person. Remember, our battle is with the spirits operating through the person. If we answer a spiritual attack with a carnal or fleshly response, we are guaranteed to lose. Ephesians 6:11 teaches us how to respond:

> *"Put on the whole armour of God, that ye may be able to stand against the wiles of the devil."*

Here's a quick summary of the armor of God as outlined in Ephesians 6:14-18:

- Truth
- Righteousness
- Gospel of Peace
- Faith
- Salvation
- Word of God
- Prayer (I like to include this one from verse 18).

These are the weapons we need to engage any enemy in spiritual warfare. As you walk along this Christian journey, you will encounter people who'll attack you every chance they get. They will malign your name. They will gossip about you. They may try to make your life as miserable as possible. Don't make the mistake of engaging with the person in the flesh. The outcome won't work out well for you. Instead, Overcomers stand on Ephesians 6:12, putting on the full armor of God

## 25 Keys to Walking Victoriously

(Ephesians 6:13-18). And remember God loves your adversary as much as He loves you.

# Overcomer

## *KEY 19 - ISAIAH 61:3*

**"To appoint unto them that mourn in Zion, to give unto them beauty for ashes, the oil of joy for mourning, the garment of praise for the spirit of heaviness; that they might be called trees of righteousness, the planting of the Lord, that he might be glorified."**

Before I start this chapter, I must emphasize this verse is how God delivered me from depression. Deliverance through scripture and prayer is my personal testimony. Remember, everyone receives deliverance, breakthrough, or healing in different ways. If you're suffering from depression, I urge you to see your doctor and follow his/her instructions.

In 1992, soon after my son Joshua was born, the doctor diagnosed me with depression. By then, I had buried my premature son, Anthony (1988), and my mother (1989). I was miserable. I went to my doctor and told her I was experiencing overwhelming sadness. She told me I had a textbook case of depression. She prescribed Zoloft and sent me on my way.

I took the medicine for maybe a week or two and then stopped because I didn't want to depend on a drug for happiness. Over the next six years or so, I went through a divorce, filed bankruptcy, and dealt with my depression as best as I could. I often sat in my apartment with all the lights off crying. I contemplated suicide but was too afraid to follow through. There was nothing good in the world, and God hated me. At least that's how I felt and what I thought.

One day, I was reading *The Battlefield of the Mind* by Joyce Meyer, and she quoted Isaiah 61:3 and explained the spirit of heaviness was depression. I said, "Does the Bible really have a verse about depression?" and grabbed my Bible. I turned to the verse and read it over and over again.

I read my Bible in a practical manner. I'm always looking for down-to-earth ways to apply what I've learned. I thought to myself, "Hold up...so are you saying depression is a heaviness and I can put on the garment of praise to overcome it?" That was my understanding of the verse. I looked at the word garment and thought, "Hmmm a garment...like a sweater or some other article of clothing. I can put praise on, and I can take praise off. If I put the praise garment on, the spirit of heaviness has to leave. If I take the praise garment off, I leave myself vulnerable to the spirit of heaviness." I was a babe in Christ, and this is the way

## *Overcomer*

I understood and processed the verse. I purposed in my heart I would praise the Lord.

Praising the Lord was hard initially. I was worried about people in the church looking at me (wow, I can't believe I actually cared about people watching me in church back then). I wondered if I looked stupid. I also thought I was too overweight to praise the Lord freely in church (many busty women know what I'm talking about so don't judge me - these thoughts went through my mind) and so I would praise the Lord at home but sit quietly in church.

I wanted to praise the Lord publicly, but insecurity stopped me. I wanted to shout and dance and sing and laugh but I would either sit or perform my simple two-step and clap my hands, nothing to bring attention to myself.

I noticed the more I praised God at home, in my car, in private, the easier to praise Him in church. The more I praised Him, the happier I became, and depression faded. I had a more positive outlook. I was optimistic instead of pessimistic. I saw good instead of only bad. And I started to believe God had a plan for my life (Jeremiah 29:11).

Perhaps you are struggling with depression like I was. If you are, I want you to put this book down and call your doctor. I want you to follow his or her instructions. And I want to ask you how much you're praising the Lord. Are you praising Him in your alone time? Are you worshiping Him? Are you pouring out your heart before Him? Are you trusting the Lord?

I recognize everyone is different and I know everyone receives healing and deliverance by various methods, but I believe with all my heart Isaiah 61:3 will help you overcome depression the way it helped me.

You don't have to be depressed. Depression is not God's will for your life. You can have happiness and joy and peace. You can enjoy life. You are not your mistakes. Your mistakes don't have to be prophetic. Your mistakes aren't necessarily indicative of your future nor your identity. You can rise above your problems. You can rise above your past. You can rise above the trials, tests, and temptations you've suffered.

I challenge you to praise the Lord. Praise Him when times are good. Praise Him when times are bad. Praise Him when you're experiencing abundance. Praise Him when you're experiencing lack. Don't stop praising Him.

Praising the Lord helped me fight during my breast cancer journey. I was intentional with my praise. I celebrated Jesus, regardless what the outcome would be. I knew praising the Lord would help me combat the scary thoughts overwhelming my mind.

## *Overcomer*

I dare not make light of what you're going through. I don't want to seem unrealistic. I know how difficult overcoming depression can be, but I believe the Word of God. I believe God can heal and deliver us using unconventional methods. Don't believe me? Let's ask Naaman.

Do you remember Naaman's story in 2 Kings 5? The Bible teaches Naaman was a Syrian soldier and a *"mighty man in valour, but he was a leper,"* (2 Kings 5:1). To make a long story short, Naaman heard about a prophet in Israel who could heal his leprosy. Naaman went to Elisha, the prophet, and was instructed to wash seven times in the Jordan river (see 2 Kings 5:10).

Naaman wasn't happy with those instructions and went away angry. Thank God, his servants were men of wisdom. They convinced him to try Elisha's method, and he dipped himself seven times in the Jordan river. Praise the Lord, *"…and his flesh came again like unto the flesh of a little child, and he was clean,"* (2 Kings 5:14). Imagine what would have happened if Naaman ignored his servants. Naaman would have remained a leper. Instead, he heeded wise instruction and received the healing and deliverance he so desperately needed.

God heals by both conventional and unconventional methods. If He healed Namaan by the dirty Jordan River, then

He can heal you from depression in unconventional ways as well. When I found out cancer had entered my body, I kept praying God would heal me miraculously. I made up my mind how my healing was going to come, and I rejected anything else. I tried to rationalize with God: "Lord, imagine the testimony I will have when I can tell people you healed me without chemotherapy. People will know the power of God." To be honest, I wasn't so much concerned with boasting in God; I was afraid of taking chemo and losing my hair!

The Lord comforted me in Starbucks the morning before my first infusion and told me to take chemo. He promised me He would control the side effects and my experience on chemo wouldn't be as bad as I anticipated. God kept His promise to me. While the side effects weren't a walk in the park, neither were they as bad as I thought they were going to be. I still have a testimony about God healing me. He healed me differently than what I wanted or liked.

What about you? Could praising the Lord be one of the tools the Lord wants to use to bring you out of depression with a strong right hand?

Overcomers have gotten to a place where they allow God to move in their lives in whichever manner He desires. Remember, Overcomers place their faith in the power of God.

## *Overcomer*

My faith was not in chemo. My faith was in God's power, His strength, His ways. Place your faith in God's power too. Always remember God *"...is able to do exceeding abundantly above all that we ask or think...,"* (Ephesians 3:20). Trust Him!

## KEY 20 - 2 TIMOTHY 1:7

**"For God hath not given us the spirit of fear; but of power, and of love, and of a sound mind."**

I mentioned in an earlier chapter how God used this verse to help me overcome the fear of my first chemo treatment. God has used this, as well as many other verses, to help me overcome fear in general. As I look back over my life, I see a scaredy cat. I see someone who allowed fear to rule her life in so many areas; it's a miracle I could break free. To be honest, I still contend with fear. I've had to apply all the lessons in this book to keep fear at bay. And because fear has been such a huge adversary, I want to spend some time on the topic.

Fear does not come from God, but it's 100% real nonetheless. Don't let anybody convince you fear isn't real. Yes, fear is real. However, fear only has the power you give it. Fear attacks everybody, but some people press through fear to accomplish their dreams and goals while others let fear render

## *Overcomer*

them stagnated, unproductive, and ineffective. Which one are you? If you're reading this book, I'm going to assume you're in the second category. You've had some successes in your life, but fear usually stops you in your tracks when you're trying to grow. Am I right?

What is fear? The definition of fear as used in 2 Timothy 1:7 is timidity, fearfulness, cowardice. Let's take a brief look at some of those definitions:

Timidity is lacking in self-assurance, courage, or bravery; easily alarmed; characterized by or indicating fear.[13] Fearfulness is apt to cause fear, feeling fear, dread, apprehension, or solicitude[14]. Cowardice means lacking courage to face danger, difficulty, opposition, pain, etc[15].

So, what does fear look like? The answer depends upon whom you ask. To be clear, I am not a psychiatrist nor a psychologist. I'm only a woman who has spent time with God. I'm a woman who always asks God why I behave the way I behave. I believe He has given me insight into this topic.

Fear has manifested itself in my life in many ways as low self-esteem, insecurity, procrastination, shame, negative

---

[13] www.dictionary.com/browse/timidity
[14] www.dictionary.com/browse/fearfulness
[15] www.dictionary.com/browse/cowardice

thinking, doubt, and indecisiveness. Fear also shows up in real physiological ways such as an upset stomach, shaky hands, and a flushed face when called upon to speak in public.

As I said, you can dress fear up in fancy names (timid, cowardice, dread, apprehension solicitude), but it's fear nonetheless, and all these words come to render you unproductive, unfruitful, and ineffective in the kingdom of God. This isn't God's will for His children.

God's will for us is power, love, and a sound mind. The definition of power is force, miraculous power, ability, abundance, and strength. I'm convinced many Christians don't know or understand the power residing in them in the person of the Holy Spirit. We are a force to be reckoned with. We have miraculous power. We have untapped abilities. We have abundance and strength. We have all of these attributes because God gave them to us. We house the power we need to combat the fear attacking us.

We also have God's agape love. A person who knows they're loved is a confident person. Christians should be the most confident people on the planet because we have the love of the Creator. We understand God loved us so much that while we were still sinners Christ died for us (see Romans 5:8).

## *Overcomer*

Knowing how much we are loved is a spiritual weapon against the forces attacking our minds and hearts with fear.

In these verses, Paul tells Timothy the spirit of fear does not originate from God. He tells Timothy in addition to power and love, God has also given him a sound mind. Strong's defines a sound mind as discipline or self-control[16]. Self-control, or temperance, is also a fruit of the spirit (see Galatians 5:23). Although the enemy will attack us with fear, we don't have to let fear dictate our actions. We are powerful. We are loved. We have self-control. We can't control what happens to us, but we can certainly control our reactions. We can choose to let fear stop us or we can choose to march forward in obedience to God's Word. The choice is ours.

Everyone has fear. Being afraid of stepping outside our comfort zone seems to be a part of human nature. Everyone becomes afraid or gets nervous or anxious. Although God understands our desire to stay within our comfort zones, we are still called to obey His commands.

Fear is a bully. Bullies use intimidation to control. Fear likes to control you as well. The Lord could be speaking to your

---

[16] Strong's Numbers G4995

heart, but fear will cause you to turn a deaf ear to the Lord and ignore His instructions. Fear will also cause you to move ahead of God and obey its instructions, rather than God's. Either of those scenarios will lead you down a path you don't want to travel, the path of disobedience and rebellion.

One of the best ways to overcome fear is obedience. Obedience will help you conquer fear every time the bully raises its head. Obedience says, "Regardless how fearful or afraid or nervous I am, I'm going to obey God." Joyce Meyer wrote a book entitled "Do it Afraid." The title alone, resonated within me and stuck with me many years after I read it.

I've always had a fear of public speaking. I remember being in maybe the 8th grade and receiving a "D" in English because I would not read my book reports aloud. I believe I told the teacher something like, "I will never read those reports," to which she replied, "Then you will fail my class." Fortunately for me, I passed all the other assignments; therefore, she couldn't fail me. I wrote the book reports, but I wouldn't read them aloud before my classmates.

The fear of public speaking followed me into high school and subsequently into the workplace. I wouldn't speak up in meetings. I would wait until the meetings were over and then go to my boss and tell him what I was too afraid to say in the

*Overcomer*

meeting. I wouldn't apply for certain positions because they required public speaking.

Eventually, I found myself saved and attending church. One day, one of the ministers told me God was calling me to be a Bible teacher. I remember saying, "I don't know who you've been talking to you, but you are wrong. I'm not speaking before a crowd of people." I was willing to disobey God to obey fear.

I ran from my calling for a long time after it became clear the Lord was calling me to teach. I saw potential Bible lessons everywhere. I always kept notebooks with me in which I'd record useful notes and tidbits. I also soon discovered I possessed a writing talent. Writing tasks which were difficult for others were easy for me, especially expounding on scriptures and stories from the Bible.

I remember when the Pastor of the church asked me to lead the singles ministry, which meant I'd have to teach a class at least once a month. I took so long giving him an answer he extended the offer to someone else. He asked me again when the other person said no. This time I said yes. I did it afraid. I was so nervous, I was literally shaking while I taught.

God was growing me up. A short time afterward, I was asked to start teaching adult Bible study. I was more nervous about teaching the adult Bible class than the singles class because Bible study required me to teach every week. I would take a deep breath and try to teach the entire lesson off one breath. The fear was awful, but everyone always complimented me and told me I was a natural teacher. I have now been teaching the Word of God for about 20 years. And guess what...I still get nervous, and my stomach still churns whenever I have to preach. Those emotions, tied to fear, still attack but I've learned obedience is the key.

Although I'm nervous before every Bible lesson, women's lesson, or sermon, I've made up my mind I will preach and teach anyway. And it never ceases to amaze me that as soon as I have the microphone in my hand and my notes are lying on the podium in front of me, the power of Almighty God endues me and pushes me with boldness to deliver what He has given me for the people. I go into a zone when I'm preaching or teaching and could preach and teach forever. I can clearly hear God's voice speaking to me, telling me what to say and how to convey His message. I remember scriptures I couldn't remember before (I've always struggled with memorization and chemo brain has made memorizing scriptures worse). I often watch the clock while I'm preaching because I could go on and on. Imagine that, the person who was afraid to preach and teach is now known as the long-winded preacher/teacher. God has a sense of humor.

## *Overcomer*

Fear still tries to make me disobey God, but I refuse to let fear stop me. I love teaching now. Teaching the Word of God, which filled me with fear and dread all those years ago, now fills me with joy and peace. I wouldn't have known joy and peace in teaching if I'd let fear have its way. How many opportunities have you missed because fear influenced you to say no instead of saying yes?

How would your life change if you stepped out in faith and obeyed God? Listen, my face still turns beet red sometimes when I'm teaching. I sometimes lose my spot in my notes. I still have worrisome dreams in which I'm standing before a crowd and can't find the scriptures in the Bible (I have that dream before every sermon). I conquer fear through obedience to God and so can you. You have to DO what you're afraid to do.

Let me give you another example before I end this section. I started writing about 18-20 years ago, around the same time I started hearing the call to teach. I started writing out Bible lessons and sermons although I wasn't yet preaching or teaching. The pastor told me, "Aretha, I see you writing books and holding conferences based upon those books." Unfortunately, I was too afraid to publish my writings because I didn't think my writing was good enough. I now have tons of unfinished projects on my hard drive. I have ideas for Christian fiction, devotionals, and Bible studies. I was too afraid to pursue publication.

In May 2016, the Lord gave me the idea to start a blog. "Wait - you mean put my writings on the internet so the entire world can see them? What if they sound stupid? What if my grammar or punctuation is wrong? What if I write the wrong word, using 'complement' instead of 'compliment'?" The Lord didn't let up. He didn't say, "You're right Aretha. Your writing isn't good, so you don't have to create the blog." Instead, He kept prompting me to publish my writings, going as far as sharing with me the importance of writing. The Lord told me He also is a writer. The passion for writing puts the Christian writer in good company!

I stepped out in obedience to the Lord and launched my blog on June 1, 2016. Since then, I've met many Christian bloggers; women like me who love the Lord, love writing, and want to encourage others through their writing. I'm experiencing an excitement, joy, and peace I never knew before because I finally obeyed Him. Writing is an outlet for me. Encouraging women is an outlet for me. Obeying God is safety for me.

I want you to step out in obedience to the Lord now. Stop putting off what He's requiring of you. Stop waiting for the

## *Overcomer*

perfect moment. If you wait for the perfect moment to obey God, fear will make sure the perfect moment never arrives. Besides, the perfect moment to obey God is NOW!

Overcoming my insecurities has been difficult but I've found the more I obey God, the easier it becomes to obey Him and overcome the symptoms of fear. Low self-esteem, procrastination, rejection, shame, doubt...all these are real in the lives of many of God's children. We know God has called us to perform a particular work, but the fear renders us disobedient, ineffective, and unproductive. God desires we produce much fruit. Fear is sent by the enemy to prevent us from producing fruit for the Lord.

Fear also prevents us from enjoying life. How can you obey the Lord with joy when fear has you in bondage? We should enjoy serving the Lord. Although I had a fear of preaching before a congregation (my face still turns red sometimes), I enjoy preaching. I love expounding on the Word of God. I also love writing. Developing a fear of sharing my writings with people only makes sense. Satan didn't want me to share them because someone would experience healing and deliverance through my writing.

Fear will keep you stuck in circumstances which are less than God's perfect plan for your life. Instead of stepping out in faith, fear will tell you to stay in an abusive relationship or dead-end job, rationalizing a relationship with an abusive man is preferable to being alone, and a dead-end job is more comfortable than applying for your dream job and facing possible rejection. I understand...I get it.

I wonder how many people aren't living up to their potential and calling because of fear. I wonder how many Christians are coming to church every Sunday with a smile on their faces, but not in their hearts. These people are miserable because they're being pulled to try something new, but the fear bully is whispering in their ears persuading them that trying is a waste of time.

Some people I've come across are popping in my mind as I type this and I realize many of the "haters" in our lives aren't hating on us, they're hating on themselves. It's difficult to be optimistic for yourself when the fear bully is breathing down your neck. Haters hate because they're too afraid to step out in faith and chase their dreams. Therefore, they become frustrated when they see their family and friends successfully chasing their dreams and goals. Deep within themselves, they wish they had the courage to realize their potential, but they're afraid.

Fear is one of the easiest and quickest ways to become discouraged. The words discouraged and encouraged both

## *Overcomer*

contain the root word "courage". Courage is defined as the quality of the mind or spirit that enables a person to face difficulty, danger, pain, etc., without fear; bravery[17]. Discouraged means you are deprived of courage, hope, or confidence[18]. Encouraged means to inspire with courage, spirit or confidence[19]. The person who's behaving as a hater toward you has probably been discouraged from stepping out in faith.

*"Be strong and <u>courageous</u>, for you shall give this people possession of the land which I swore to their fathers to give them. Only be strong and very <u>courageous</u>; be careful to do according to all the law which Moses My servant commanded you; do not turn from it to the right or to the left, so that you may have success wherever you go," (Joshua 1:6-7, NASB).*

*"Have I not commanded you? Be strong and courageous! Do not tremble or be dismayed, for the Lord your God is with you wherever you go," (Joshua 1:9, NASB).*

Three verses…three instances in which God commanded Joshua to be courageous. Why? Moses was dead, and the responsibility of leading the children of Israel into the promised

---

[17] www.dictionary.com/browse/courage
[18] www.dictionary.com/browse/discourage
[19] www.dictionary.com/browse/encourage

land shifted to Joshua. I can imagine Joshua was feeling overwhelmed and unqualified for the job. All this time he'd been Moses' helper. Joshua hadn't been in charge, and now God was telling Joshua about the awesome task set before him. Joshua was about to take on a major undertaking. Although he was a fighter, he was feeling intimidated. Maybe he wondered whether God would defend and protect him the same way He defended and protected Moses. I infer this about Joshua because God knows our thoughts afar off and one of the statements God made to Joshua was, *"...Just as I have been with Moses, I will be with you; I will not fail you or forsake you,"* (Joshua 1:5, NASB). Imagine for a moment you're Joshua. How would you feel?

I know exactly how I'd feel, I'd tell God to choose somebody else, someone experienced, someone more prepared. Despite how Joshua felt in his flesh, he obeyed the Lord's voice. He stepped out in faith, and God is requiring the same of you and me.

Joshua assumed the leadership role God granted him, and he completed the assignments laid before him. He trusted God. Joshua had faith in God and God did exactly what He promised Joshua. Joshua didn't need to fear anything or anybody because

## *Overcomer*

God was with him and neither should we fear anything or anybody because He is with us too.

We can be confident God will accomplish exactly what He promised He would accomplish in our lives. We need to be obedient and courageous like Joshua. Although we're facing insurmountable odds and don't know how we're going to complete the tasks before us, we have to be courageous and step out in faith. We have to trust God. We have to remember what He did for Moses, Joshua, and others. Overcomer's faith says since God came through for them, she can be confident He will come through for her too. Do you believe He will come through for you?

# 25 Keys to Walking Victoriously

## KEY 21 - PSALM 23:4

**"Yea, though I walk through the valley of the shadow of death, I will fear no evil: for thou art with me; thy rod and thy staff they comfort me."**

Dealing with hardships, obstacles, challenges (whatever you want to call them) is difficult. Not knowing how long they're going to last makes enduring them more difficult. When financial crises, health issues, or marital strife occurs, we feel as though we're going to have to contend with the issue forever. We can't see an end. The only thing you can see is the battle currently before you. You can't see the win. You can't see the victory. You can't see the celebration because you're so focused on the fear, confusion, and heartache you're experiencing.

Psalm 23:4 has given me comfort over the years as it reminds me I'm only walking *"...through the valley..."* Staying in the valley, in the shadow of death, isn't God's will for me. God's will is for me to come out the other side of the valley

## *Overcomer*

victorious, giving Him praise, glory, and honor. Let's take a look at Jesus' example of how to endure life's storms when they seemingly arise from out of nowhere.

*"Now it came to pass on a certain day, that He went into a ship with His disciples: and He said unto them, 'Let us go over unto the other side of the lake.' And they launched forth. But as they sailed He fell asleep: and there came down a storm of wind on the lake; and they were filled with water and were in jeopardy. And they came to him, and awoke Him, saying, 'Master, master, we perish.' Then He arose, and rebuked the wind and the ranging of the water: and they ceased, and there was a calm. And He said unto them, 'Where is your faith?' And they being afraid wondered, saying one to another, 'What manner of man is this! For He commandeth even the winds and water, and they obey him,'" (Luke 8:22-25).*

Have you ever gone through a storm, a trial, which was so tumultuous it made you feel as though you were going to perish? Those types of storms seem to last forever. Regardless how much you pray, study the Bible, and fast, the storm doesn't relent. On the contrary, the storm only seems to intensify. What's an Overcomer to do? Have faith!

Verse 22 of this story records Jesus telling the disciples what the end of their trip on the ship was going to be. He said,

## 25 Keys to Walking Victoriously

*"Let us go over unto the other side of the lake."* Although Jesus told them the destination and they heard Him, they seem to have forgotten what He said when the storm came because they woke Him saying they were going to perish.

Now, before I continue, I want to make a point. A few chapters ago, I emphasized the importance of seeking a Word from the Lord. Receiving a Word from Him is important because it gives the foundation upon which to stand when we're facing various trials. Jesus gave them a Word in this story. The Word was they were going to the other side of the lake.

Are you currently going through a trial, a storm? Has the Lord given you a Word of comfort, encouragement, or instruction? If so, stand on the Word. If not, seek the Lord for instructions and then stand on the Word.

As I type this chapter, I'm going through a storm. The winds are howling, the rain is pouring, and I can't see a victory with my natural eye. However, the Word the Lord keeps speaking to me is to trust Him to bring me out in due season. By faith, I'm trusting God to keep me during the storm. If I look at the storm raging around me, I will end up going to Jesus like the disciples saying, "Lord, I'm about to perish."

I need you to stand on the promises of God. Stop looking at your circumstances. Stop looking at what's going on around

*Overcomer*

you. I know the storm is difficult and I know you're wondering how long the storm is going to last. Remember, you're going "through" a storm. God is not going to leave you in the storm. Hold on and trust Him.

Overcomers aren't immune to trials. They don't get a special pass. They experience fear, uncertainty, and moments of doubt like everybody else. However, Overcomers know if they stay focused on the storm raging around them, they will faint.

*"But the ship was now in the midst of the sea, tossed with waves: for the wind was contrary. And in the fourth watch of the night Jesus went unto them, walking on the sea. And when the disciples saw Him walking on the sea, they were troubled, saying, It is a spirit; and they cried out for fear. But straightway Jesus spake unto them, saying, Be of good cheer; it is I; be not afraid. And Peter answered Him and said, Lord if it be thou, bid me come unto thee on the water," (Matthew 14:24-28).*

Peter experienced another storm with Jesus. Notice, before Peter asked to join Jesus on the water, the storm was already brewing, and the wind was already "contrary." The disciples were afraid when they saw Jesus, but He spoke a word: *"Be of good cheer; it is I; be not afraid."* Peter grabbed hold of those words and, regardless the storm raging around them, asked to join Jesus on the water. I think it speaks volumes Peter would rather be on the water with Jesus, exposed to the elements, than on the ship without Him.

How about you? Would you rather be comfortable without Jesus or in a storm with Him? The storm may be scarier, but I'd rather leave everybody else and join Him in the midst of the storm because only He can speak to storms, subsequently calming them. God will calm your storms. Stay focused on His promises.

Overcomers stay focused on God's ability, His power. Overcomers have the attitude which says although I'm going through right now and can't see how God is going to deliver me, I know He is able. And knowing He is able fills them with encouragement to endure.

Yes, the valley of the shadow of death is real. Storms are real. Trials are real. Hardships and challenges are real. Many people will face illnesses and financial setbacks. But we serve a mighty God who is able to rebuke the situations we're facing and create immediate calm.

"Where is your faith?" Jesus spoke those words to the disciples, and He's speaking those words to us today.

# Overcomer

### *KEY 22 - JOB 2:10*

**"But he said unto her, Thou speakest as one of the foolish women speaketh. What? Shall we receive good at the hand of God, and shall we not receive evil? In all this did not Job sin with his lips."**

Evil, infirmities, reproaches, necessities, persecutions, distress, and hardships are going to come. If you live long enough, you will endure more hardships than you ever expected. They're going to happen. What will your attitude be when or if they happen to you?

You may be familiar with Job's story. A conversation was held in heaven between God and Satan. God mentioned Job's name saying, *"Hast thou considered my servant Job, that there is none like him in the earth, a perfect and upright man, one that feareth God, and escheweth evil?"* (Job 1:8). Satan replied basically saying, "Of course he fears you. You've spoiled him." God challenged Satan saying he could afflict Job, but couldn't touch Job's body. Satan destroyed all Job's livestock and had all his children killed. Job didn't sin against God.

God and Satan had yet another conversation in which Satan told God Job would curse him if God allowed Satan to touch Job's body. God told Satan he could touch Job's body, but he couldn't kill him. The Bible records Satan afflicted Job's body with *"...boils from the sole of his foot unto his crown,"* (Job 2:7). After this incident Job's wife said, *"Dost thou still retain thine integrity? Curse God, and die,"* to which Job responded with *"...shall we receive good at the hand of God, and shall we not receive evil?"* (Job 2:9-10). Christians need to have the same attitude toward God. Unfortunately, many of us can only retain our integrity when life is going well. We need to get to a place where we walk in integrity despite of what we're going through.

Integrity is defined as adherence to moral and ethical principles; soundness of moral character; honesty[20]. In other words, integrity is sticking to a holy and righteous lifestyle although you're being severely tried and tested. Integrity is standing with God when everything going on around you is

---

[20] www.dictionary.com/browse/integrity

*Overcomer*

telling you to stand against Him, to blame Him, to disobey Him, to curse Him and die.

When I was younger in my Christian walk, I often resorted to ungodly thinking, decisions, and behaviors when I faced hard times. You know how children have tantrums in the grocery store or toy store when they see something they want but their parents won't buy it for them? That was me. If I asked God for something and He didn't provide it, I would throw a temper tantrum. Or if God allowed hard times into my life, I'd fall out like a child falls out, kicking my feet, crying and screaming.

"Why me, God? Why me?" would be my cry. Thoughts ranging from God doesn't exist, to a loving God wouldn't allow this to happen to me, to my life was better before I accepted Jesus Christ as my Lord and Savior, popped in my mind. When such discouraging thoughts popped into my head, ungodly decisions and behaviors would soon follow. I think Paul summed up my vicious cycle when he wrote, *"When I was a child, I spake as a child, I understood as a child, I thought as a child: but when I became a man, I put away childish things,"* (1 Corinthians 13:11). I had to grow up.

Adults have to face disappointments like adults. We can't fall out and throw temper tantrums every time life deals us complications. We have to take care of our children although bills are past due. We have to go to work although we dislike our bosses or coworkers. We have to clean our homes even if we have a backache. We have to be cordial to people when they're disagreeable. Putting this in a spiritual context, mature Christians have to handle kingdom business even when their lives are falling apart around them. We can't come off the battlefield because one of our children is acting up. We don't get to come off the battlefield because we've had a death in the family. We have to press forward. We have to keep praising the Lord. We have to keep trusting and believing Him for victory in all areas of our lives although it may look like nothing good is going on for us.

Job didn't sin against God. He was an Overcomer. We are Overcomers too. Yes, we may become discouraged, sad, or depressed. Yes, we may question God. Yes, we may wonder "why me?" We may feel like giving up. We can't let any of those thoughts move us to disobey God. We have to be resolute in knowing God will bring us out. Let's take a look at Job 27:2-5.

*"As God liveth, who hath taken away my judgment; and the Almighty, who hath vexed my soul; All the while my breath is in me, and the spirit of God is in my nostrils; my lips shall not*

## *Overcomer*

*speak wickedness, nor my tongue utter deceit. God forbid that I should justify you: till I die I will not remove mine integrity from me."*

Imagine being able to utter these words, *"...till I die I will not remove mine integrity from me,"* (KJV). Job doesn't say his integrity only holds as long as life is going well. Instead, he says as long as he's alive he will hold on to his integrity. He will not turn his back on God. He will not speak against Him. He will not dishonor Him. Job is definitely an Overcomer. He faced the hardest tests I've ever seen, and yet he stood. He maintained his integrity.

What about you? Will you maintain your integrity? Will you hold on to God's hand and refuse to let go? Stand fast in your faith. Focus on the love of God instead of the pain you're experiencing. One day, someone will speak of your integrity the way we speak of Job's.

## KEY 23 - ISAIAH 40:31

**"But they that wait upon the Lord shall renew their strength; they shall mount up with wings as eagles; they shall run, and not be weary; and they shall walk, and not faint."**

Any book written about overcoming obstacles which doesn't include Isaiah 40:31 is lacking.

About nine years ago, I went to work one fall morning only to learn I, along with a bunch of my co-workers, was being laid off. My employer was nice enough to keep us on for two weeks during which time we were instructed to spend our days looking for new jobs. I spent the first day stressed, looking for a new job, because I'd bought a house the previous November and had a hefty mortgage I still needed to pay, along with all my other bills.

## *Overcomer*

As I was driving on the highway on my way home, I prayed to the Lord expressing my concerns when I pulled alongside a tractor-trailer with Isaiah 40:31 written on the back. I smiled to myself and said, "Ok, Lord, I hear you."

The church I was attending had recently rented a small space in which to have services, but the space needed a lot of work. When my two weeks was up with the company, I started spending my days at the new church building cleaning and painting and daydreaming about all the services we were going to have.

The word "wait" in Isaiah 40:31 means to gather (together), look, patiently, tarry, wait (for, on, upon)[21]. While I waited on the Lord to help me find a new job, I decided to wait (serve) on Him by helping to prepare our new church building. I refused to sit around feeling sorry for myself.

We have a choice when we face trouble: we can become paralyzed with fear or step out in faith in service to the Lord. Regardless our decision, the length of time we spend in trouble is going to come and go. Let's say your trouble comes and stays 14 days. You can spend those 14 days worried out of your mind

---

[21] Strong's Numbers H6960

or relaxed in the Father's arms. Regardless of how you spend the time, you have to go through the 14 days.

I chose to spend the time I was laid off serving the Lord. Did I worry? Yes, but I took my worry, my concern, my anxiety to the new church and painted walls, cleaned the kitchen, and helped hang curtains. While I waited (tarried) patiently for the Lord, I also waited (served) on Him. What are you doing in the midst of your trouble? How are you waiting?

Isaiah 40:31 contains a promise for Overcomers:

*"Yet those who wait for the Lord will gain new strength; They will mount up with wings like eagles, They will run and not get tired, They will walk and not become weary," (NASB).*

Those promises only come to those who wait on Him. Hence the reason I emphasized the waiting part of the verse first is this chapter.

Everyone who faces a storm, a trial, a test, or any type of trouble will soon become weary (see verses 28-30). We all want to give up sometimes. Don't believe anyone who says they've never wanted to give up. Don't believe anyone who says they're strong all the time. NO! We all grow tired. God will renew our strength when we grow weary. When we get tired and weary, the Lord graces us with newness, new zeal, more endurance. Or, what I call my second wind.

We need to see our trouble from the eagle's vantage point. Most people only see the situation from the ground view. The ground view is chaotic, confusing, scary, and overwhelming. The eagle's viewpoint is not. When you wait on the Lord, you're able to mount up on wings like an eagle. An eagle can soar above the storm. An eagle uses the winds to keep him in the air. He doesn't have to flap his wings hard because the wind keeps him moving. The winds in your storm can keep you airborne, high above your problems and circumstances when you place your faith, hope, and trust in God. Waiting on the Lord gives you the ability to see your situation from a different vantage point. You're able to see the bigger picture.

Keep waiting on the Lord, and He will give you the ability to run when everyone else becomes weary and too tired to press on. You'll be able to walk when everyone else faints. You'll be able to endure longer and accomplish more because you're not performing for the Lord in your flesh but by the Spirit.

*"Watch and pray, that ye enter not into temptation: the spirit indeed is willing, but the flesh is weak," (Matthew 26:41).*

## 25 Keys to Walking Victoriously

Jesus spoke these words to His disciples when they were in the Garden of Gethsemane. The disciples were asleep when they should have been praying. Their flesh overtook them, and they fell asleep. Your flesh will always overtake you if you're not careful. If you want to be able to endure, you have to strengthen your spirit. Waiting on the Lord is one of the best ways to gain strength.

You are stronger than you know. You can overcome any trouble you face when you cast your care upon Him. Casting your care upon God enables you to receive the strength you need to persevere in life's trials. Purpose in your heart to wait as an Overcomer, trusting Isaiah 40:31.

*Overcomer*

## *KEY 24 - 1 PETER 5:7*

**"Casting all your care upon Him; for He careth for you."**

God is concerned about you. He cares about what happens to you. He cares what people say about you. He cares about the trouble you're in. He cares about every tear you shed. He cares about the consequences of the sins you commit.

He understands we are flesh and blood and have feelings and emotions. He knows we're easily frightened. He knows we become emotional and upset. He knows we ache inside when a loved one dies. God knows we're prone to hold stress in our bodies, leading to sickness. And because He is concerned about our well-being, the Lord tells us to cast all our care on Him because He cares for us.

What has you concerned right now? What's keeping you up at night full of anxiety? Throw it on the Lord? Which of your children has you stressed? Cast him or her upon the Lord. How many of your bills are behind? Cast them upon Jesus.

The Bible tells us to cast all our care on Him. All means all, not holding any back. At the time I'm typing this, I have a lot of concerns for myself and my loved ones. I'm concerned about my job. I'm concerned about this book - will it be well-received, will the readers find spelling, grammar, or punctuation mistakes? I'm concerned about my best friend's son who's in the hospital. I'm concerned about one of my brothers. I'm concerned about my son and his daughter. I'm concerned about my daughter going to high school in the fall.

Instead of holding on to those concerns and letting them stress me out, I'm invited to cast them, throw them, upon the Lord because He cares for me. God is interested in everything concerning you and me, and He wants us to trust Him.

I love seeing how Jesus was moved with compassion for people in the Bible. Let's take a look at a few examples.

> *"And Jesus went forth, and saw a great multitude, and was moved with compassion toward them, and He healed their sick," (Matthew 14:14).*

## *Overcomer*

Jesus cared about their illnesses, so He healed them. He sees your illness as well. Going through a life-threatening illness can leave you feeling lonely. You feel like no one understands nor cares about what you're going through. God cares. He was moved with compassion in Matthew 14:14 because he cared and He's moved with compassion today because He cares for us. Overcomers know God cares about them. Although they often feel alone, they know they aren't. As we discussed previously, Overcomers try not to get caught up in their emotions. Instead, they try to stand upon the word of God.

*"Then Jesus called His disciples unto Him, and said, I have compassion on the multitude, because they continue with me now three days, and have nothing to eat: and I will not send them away fasting, lest they faint in the way, (Matthew 15:32).*

A multitude of people followed Jesus for three days. He knew they were hungry and He cared. He refused to send the multitude away without feeding them. Christ has not changed. He's still feeding us today. He refuses to send us away hungry. He desires we have the spiritual and physical food we need. Why? Because He cares about us. What an awesome Savior we serve!

# 25 Keys to Walking Victoriously

*"So Jesus had compassion on them, and touched their eyes: and immediately their eyes received sight, and they followed Him." (Matthew 20:34).*

Perhaps you're familiar with this story. Once again, a multitude of people was following Jesus. The Bible says as He passed by, two blind men cried out to Him saying, *"Have mercy on us, O Lord, thou son of David,"* (verse 30). The multitude tried to quiet the men, but they cried out more. Jesus asked them what they wanted, and they replied they wanted sight (verses 32-33). Jesus had compassion on them, touched their eyes, and they were able to see.

Jesus' care for the people didn't stop at a feeling of pity or sympathy. No, it was greater than a simple feeling. The compassion He felt for the people compelled Him to move on behalf of the people, relieving their pain, suffering, and sorrow.

Overcomers believe God is going to eventually move on their behalf. They hope in Him. They place their faith in Him. Overcomers try to see beyond their current circumstances. They try to look ahead at the glory which shall be revealed either on this side of eternity or the other.

Do you believe God cares for you? Do you believe you can cast your cares upon Him? If yes, praise the Lord. If no, start believing today. Start casting, throwing, your cares upon Him. Although leaving the cares with Him is difficult, cast them upon Him anyway. Resist the temptation to pick up the cares again and carry them yourself when you don't see Him moving as quickly as you'd like. He said we could cast our cares upon Him and He fully expects us to cast them. Besides, He can carry our burdens much easier than we can.

*25 Keys to Walking Victoriously*

### *KEY 25 - ACTS 28:5*

**"And he shook off the beast into the fire, and felt no harm."**

We've spent a lot of time together reading and studying scriptures regarding being an Overcomer, and we've finally come to the last chapter. Before we tackle Acts 28, let me thank you right now for spending this time with me. I pray reading this book has been as much a blessing to you – as writing the book was for me.

Writing this book made me remember losses, illnesses, and hardships I'd much rather forget. The book also emphasized the importance of God's word in my life. From the moment my dad gave me my first Bible, I've been enamored with the scriptures.

The Bible is my favorite book and has brought me strength, healing, hope, comfort, deliverance, laughter, and transformation. I still have a long way to go on this journey we

## *Overcomer*

call our Christian walk. I still have lots to learn, and I still need to grow in Him. Doubt, fear, and insecurities have attached themselves to me over the years, and I've had to shake them loose one way or another. Writing this book was therapeutic as I revisited the verses and Bible stories God used to deliver me from the despair, depression, anxiety, and fear that gripped me over the years. Let's dive into this last study. Follow me as I share another freeing Bible story.

Paul and some other prisoners were sailing to Rome when, *"...a tempestuous wind, called Euroclydon,"* (Acts 27:14) arose, and the ship eventually ran aground. Everyone made it safely off the ship onto the island of Melita (Acts 28:1). They kindled a fire and Paul was gathering sticks to lay on the fire when a venomous viper came out of the heat *"...and fastened on his hand,"* (Acts 28:3). Everyone watched, waiting for Paul to die. Instead, Paul shook the viper off his hand into the fire. The Bible records Paul *"...felt no harm,"* (Acts 28:5).

Some of you have been through so much. People were watching and waiting to see if you would faint, give up, or curse God. Perhaps this describes where you are now in your walk with Christ. Maybe you feel like giving up. You're exhausted, and you don't know how you're going to make another day. Every other scripture and Bible story I provided in this book, while you acknowledge they were good, didn't minister the healing and deliverance you desperately sought and needed. If this describes you, I want to tell you to shake it off.

Some things hold on to us because we allow them to be so. Some things hold on to us because we're comfortable with them. I grew comfortable with my depression and fear as they gave me the excuses I was looking for not to pursue my dreams. I grew comfortable in my fear because it allowed me to be lazy. Fear permitted me to disobey God. Besides, God knew my heart, and He knew I was too afraid to speak before crowds or publicly share my writings. He understood what I was going through. And so, I stayed stuck right where I was.

Paul didn't give the viper opportunity to wrap itself around his arm. The viper fastened on to Paul's hand, and he immediately shook it off and felt no harm. My friend, you've been holding on to depression, despair, hatred, anger, unforgiveness, and envy so long they've become comfortable to you. Shake off any of these things that may have fastened themselves to you.

Listen, the person who hurt you may never apologize to you. We must learn to accept the apology we may never get. The person who trespassed against you may have already passed away, but you're still harboring unforgiveness in your heart toward them. You are not hurting the person. You're only hurting yourself. You have to shake unforgiveness off into the fire if you want to walk in freedom.

Some of you are angry at your spouse, and your spouse doesn't know. You're still angry your husband committed adultery. And in your own little ways, you're making him pay for the affair all these years later. Shake it off.

Perhaps some of you have a blended family, and your spouse doesn't treat your children nicely. You stayed with your spouse, and now your children are grown, and you're still angry because you're holding on to how your children were treated five, ten, fifteen years or more ago. Yet, your children love your spouse and have let go of the past. Let go of the bitterness and heal your family.

You're disappointed because your life didn't work out the way you'd always hoped. You look around and see people younger than you obtaining the blessing and favor you desired. Instead of taking your disappointment to the Lord in prayer, you're seething in anger against the younger ones whom God is blessing. You cannot curse whom God has blessed so stop trying. Shake it off and let it go.

I know your baby passed away. I know you're hurting inside. You can't move beyond, "Why me?" I know. Trust me when I tell you I know what you're feeling. I was in that place many years ago. If you need to see a therapist or trusted counselor, please see one. Your baby is enjoying eternity with God, but you're sad and depressed. Grieve as you must. Talk to your Pastor. I'm not going to tell you to let go of your memories because letting go of the death of a loved one is much too difficult. Instead, I'm going to tell you to embrace healing.

And my beautiful Sister who had the abortion, you can't seem to forgive yourself for aborting the baby. You've been walking in shame and regret all these years. You've been afraid to tell anyone about it. Perhaps you never told the father you were pregnant. Or maybe the father drove you to the abortion facility, and now you can't forgive yourself nor him. You have to forgive. You have to let go of the shame and unforgiveness, or they'll consume you. The same God who healed me of cancer can heal you of an abortion.

So, you indulged in a homosexual relationship. You've heard Christians bashing homosexuals or lesbians, and you're afraid to open up and talk to someone about your past. Or perhaps you're still experiencing those feelings now. Please seek the Lord and a trusted counselor. Your Pastor is a good resource. It's ok to speak with someone but make sure the

## *Overcomer*

person will love you through this without judgment. Shake off the shame and embarrassment.

Maybe you're like me: a cancer survivor. You're afraid of recurrence, and you can't seem to find peace as a survivor. Cancer turned your life upset down, and you're still wondering why God allowed the disease to touch your life. God may never tell you why He allowed it. You must trust His plans and purposes for your life. Instead of focusing on why He allowed the disease to touch your life, focus on why He let you survive. He wants you to accomplish a particular work for His glory. Find out what the work is and perform it. You survived cancer, don't let it steal your new life.

I could include more scenarios, but instead of typing them and making the mistake of excluding the scenario you need, I'd much rather focus on the solution to all the scenarios: Jesus Christ.

I was a miserable young woman when He pulled me out of the pit of despair in 1989. Over the next 10 years I dealt with the aftermath of both my son and my mother dying, another pregnancy, a marriage to someone I had no business marrying, a subsequent divorce, bankruptcy, fear, depression, anxiety, low self-esteem, disappointments, feelings of loneliness and hopelessness, financial problems, and despair. Since then I've also had to deal with remarriage and blended family struggles, job losses, cancer, and my brother's death. As I type this, I can tell you with assurance God has healed and/or delivered me from the negative effects of all these things. And since He did it for me, I know He will heal and deliver you too.

I'm not going to lie to you and tell you I know everything about the Bible nor everything about God. What I can tell you is I know:

He is awesome

He is my Father

He healed me

He delivered me

He has been with me every step of the way.

I don't know much - but this I know - He loves me unconditionally. And He loves you unconditionally as well. Relax in His love. Embrace His love. Find confidence and assurance in His love. Be bold in His love. Overcome with His love.

Shake off any and everything which comes to hinder your walk with Christ. Walk in the truth in the Lord Jesus Christ and be the Overcomer He came and died for you to be. You are better, stronger, and more powerful than you know. Victory, joy, and freedom are yours in Christ Jesus. And although the enemy will try you from time to time with the same things you've already overcome, standing on the Word of God will help you prevail over every attack the enemy brings.

*"...If ye continue in my Word, then are ye my disciples indeed; and ye shall know the truth, and the truth shall make you free," (John 8:32).*

Knowing what the Word of God says about you and your trial(s) empowers you to speak life and victory over yourself. The Word of God is the truth, and speaking truth is freeing. Don't let the enemy tempt you back into bondage.

*"Wherefore seeing we also are compassed about with so great a cloud of witnesses, let us lay aside every weight, and the sin which doth so easily beset us, and let us run with patience the race that is set before us," (Hebrews 12:1).*

This book includes some of the cloud of witnesses' stories who are mentioned in Hebrews 12:1. And of course, I could have included many more. Knowing their stories and being reminded of their victories encourage us to *"lay aside every weight, and the sin"* that besets (troubles, harasses, assails, surrounds) us.

Purpose in your heart and mind that you won't allow fear to control your life when fear attacks you in the future. Make the same declaration about insecurities, unforgiveness, your past, etc. Victory is yours, dear Sister. You are an Overcomer through the power, blood, life, and death of the Lord Jesus Christ.

***Don't ever forget who are you, Overcomer!***

*Overcomer*

## *CLOSING WORDS*

Before I end this book, I have to ask whether you're saved. If not, would you like to accept Jesus Christ as your Lord AND Savior? If not, the seed has been planted, and I'm praying God sends someone to water the seed, leading to your salvation. If you want to accept Christ's gift of salvation, won't you pray this prayer with me right now?

*Father, I come to You in the name of Jesus asking You to forgive me of my sins and save me. I believe in my heart that You raised Jesus from the dead and I confess with my mouth the Lord Jesus. I ask that You fill me with Your Spirit and help me to live a life that's pleasing in your sight.*
*In Jesus' name, Amen.*

If you sincerely prayed this prayer, then according to the bible, you are now saved. You are now an Overcomer. Please find and join a Bible-believing, Bible-teaching, Bible-preaching church and allow them to teach you more about the Lord.

In His service,
~Aretha Grant
1/11/18

## *25 Keys to Walking Victoriously*

To contact the author, write:
Aretha Grant
PO Box 150
Fairplay, MD 21733

Internet Address: www.arethagrant.com

I would love to hear how **Overcomer** helped you. Your prayer requests are also welcome.

Made in the USA
Coppell, TX
30 December 2022